Also by Susan Gabriel

The Secret Sense of Wildflower
(a Kirkus Reviews Best Book of 2012)

Lily's Song
(sequel to *The Secret Sense of Wildflower*)

Temple Secrets

Trueluck Summer

Grace, Grits & Ghosts: Southern Short Stories

Seeking Sara Summers

Quentin & The Cave Boy

Circle of the Ancestors

Available at all booksellers
in print, ebook and audio formats.

Fearless Writing for Women

Extreme Encouragement and Writing Inspiration

Susan Gabriel

Wild Lily Arts

Fearless Writing for Women

Copyright © 2014 by Susan Gabriel

All rights reserved. No part of this book may be reproduced or transmitted in any form or by any means without written permission of the author, except in the case of brief quotations embodied in critical articles and reviews.

Cover photograph of Shakespeare & Company Bookstore in Paris by Elena Vilalta

ISBN 978-0-9835882-5-2

Published by Wild Lily Arts

Foreword

How this book will help you become a Fearless Writer!

All writers are works-in-progress. No matter what we write or want to write we need the courage to start writing and keep going day after day. No small feat, given all the distractions we face as women who work, raise children, take care of elderly parents and otherwise run our workplaces and our homes.

Since our lives are often extreme, we need extreme encouragement and guidance in its essential elements.

In 93 selected writings, stories, lists and amazing quotes, I give you guidance and encouragement that I hope will inspire you, make you think, make you laugh and most importantly, get you writing **today**.

With seventeen years of writing experience, as well as ten years' experience as a licensed professional counselor, I know that living a creative life can be full of blessings, as well as a curse or two.

I know what it's like to question if I have anything to say.

I know what it's like to fear rejection from literary agents, publishers, critics and readers. And I also know how to persevere in spite of my fears.

My second novel, *The Secret Sense of Wildflower*—a historical, southern, coming-of-age story—received a starred review by Kirkus Reviews and was named to their list of Best Books of 2012. Yet my greatest success lies with a healthy, growing band of readers who await my next book. Readers I genuinely care about and nurture. A strong inner drive also keeps me going and a sense of purpose that won't let me quit. Fueled by inspiration, I've found a treasure trove of material to help me carry on.

This book contains my own original writings, as well as reflections on stories and quotes from well-known authors on how to live the writing life and thrive in it. It includes success stories, inspiring quotes about creativity, as well as dynamic lists that will help you start writing and keep going.

Read the entries one at a time or all at one sitting and let the message of this book work through you. Then act on the guidance. Your writing will get better and your fearlessness as a writer will grow as a result.

I use these stories in my popular Fearless Writing for Women workshops, and I hope they will inspire and encourage you to persevere through those times of your life when you need courage and resilience.

Be bold. Be honest. Be brave.

Table of Contents

Artistic Integrity: 1
Stay True to Your Story 1
Where Ideas Come From 3
Search Out Beautiful Writing 6
Girl with a Pearl Earring 7
The Art of "Shitty" First Drafts 8
What Writers Can Learn from Coyotes 10
A Lesson from Tina Fey 12
1% English Breakfast Tea 14
101 Excuses Why People Don't Write 16
Famous First Lines 22
How to Make your Life a Work of Art 24
Art is Work 25
The Magic of Fiction 26
Flannery's Secret 27
to Becoming a Great Writer 27
Poets Talk Poetry 29
Loneliness 32
Hug A Writer Day 33

An Essentially Private Business 34
Writers Who Are Also Mothers 36
A Pulitzer in Bubble Wrap? 38
Writing Later In Life 40
The Courage to Follow Your Heart 41
and Intuition 41
Kill Your Darlings 42
Encouraging Quotes about Writing 44
and the Creative Life 44
Your Writing Routine 46
Yellow Legal Pads 48
Storytelling 50
Writer's Block, Anyone? 52
The Power of Vulnerability 53
Rejection and Perseverance 56
Top 10 New Year's Resolutions 58
for Writers 58
Avoid Success at all Costs? 60
12 Quotes by Poets about Poetry 62
Writing Elf Exposed 65
The Most Difficult Job 66
You Will Ever Have 66

Revising Is About Re-visioning 68
Finding the Best Titles 70
How to Write in 700 Easy Lessons 72
Deep Conversations 74
Stopping the Divine Dance of Avoidance 76
Don't Look Back! 80
Wisdom from a Composer 80
Fabulous Quotes about 82
Writing and Creativity 82
A Choice or Chosen? 84
Secretly. Compulsively. Shyly 86
Are You Resilient? 88
Resolutions for Writers That Might Truly, Deeply Change Your Life 90
Perseverance 93
Take Wrong Turns 95
More Great Quotes about 97
Writing and Creativity 97
Attitude of Gratitude 99
Fake It Till You Make It 104
The Gift that Revives the Soul 106
Our Deepest Fear 108

Keeping the Channel Open 109
It's Never Too Late to Start 110
Your Writing Career 110
Things To Do While The Economy Sucks 112
Top 5 Tips for Aspiring Writers, Plus One 114
More Favorite Quotes about 117
Writing and Creativity 117
Muse It or Lose It 119
What Are You Missing? 122
Do You Have "Barnum In Your Bones"? 125
Follow your Bliss 127
The Place of the Artist 129
10,000 Hours 130
7 Awesome Quotes about Creativity 132
A League of Our Own 134
Dare To Compete 136
A Lesson from Harriet Tubman 138
A Different Kind of Empty Nest 140
Top 5 Favorite Quotes of All Time 142
Never Say Never 143
Defying the Odds 144
Coming Out of the Closet as a Writer 145

Life Has a Much Bigger Imagination 147
Than We Do 147
Moments of Glad Grace 150
Are You Free? 152
The Journey 153
Another 100 Things I'm Grateful For 154
What Makes You Come Alive? 159
The Incredibly Messy Process 161
of Writing a First Book 161
A Way of Life 163
What Writers and Artists Can Learn 164
from the Rocky Mountains 164
How to Stay Inspired 166
To Meander 168
Writer Spends Year Walking by River 170
A Good Rejection? 174
What Kind of Fiction Is It? 176
How Creativity Works 178
The Alchemy of Revision 180
The Tenacity of Wildflowers and Writers 184
77 Things to Do 186
When Stressed or Uninspired 186

Never. Give. Up. 191
A Blessing for Writers 194
Parting Words 195

Artistic Integrity:
Stay True to Your Story

It took my twenty-something daughter, who is wise beyond her years and has an artist's soul, to remind me of artistic integrity.

I was in a quandary over what to do with some suggestions my literary agent made, who I respect and adore, about a new manuscript I had sent her.

What I have learned over the years is that if you give a manuscript to a dozen different readers they will come up with a dozen different suggestions on how to make the story better. And what I've also learned is that there are some opinions that you trust more than others. These opinions are usually from people who are professionals (like literary agents and editors) who make a living in the service of stories and/or they are people who read a tremendous amount and intrinsically know what makes a story good.

But still, even those trusted professionals and/or avid readers sometimes say something that doesn't quite mesh with what the writer envisions. And here's where my daughter, Krista, comes in. When I confessed my latest dilemma, her advice was perfect:

"I think this one comes down to artistic integrity. These are YOUR characters, YOUR story, YOUR baby—follow your heart on this one and make sure you love the result."

Well, you can see why I'm proud. This is sage advice I can pass on to every writer and artist. Sure, there is a need to be flexible and humble and not turn down good suggestions when they are given. But you are responsible for this particular creation and to that end, your **artistic integrity** must be at the core of every decision.

So get some good input and then follow your heart.

Where Ideas Come From

A frequent question asked by my readers is: How do you come up with the ideas for your novels? All the ideas for my books and short stories have come in different ways, but the story of *The Secret Sense of Wildflower* is one of the more interesting ones.

Twelve years ago, at four in the morning, I awoke with a clear, resounding voice in my head. It was the voice of a girl who began to tell me her story: *There are two things I'm afraid of,* she said. *One is dying young. The other is Johnny Monroe.*

A day or two before, I had visited our small family cemetery located in the southern Appalachian Mountains. I spent an afternoon walking among the final resting places of my grandparents, aunts, uncles and cousins, as well as ancestors I had never known. Had I accidentally brought one of them home with me, who needed her story told?

Rest assured, mental illness does not run in my family. But for a fiction writer, to get the "voice" of a character so clearly is really good news. I, however, wanted to go back to sleep. Who wouldn't, at 4 o'clock in the morning? For a time, I debated whether or not to get up. I ultimately decided that if I didn't claim this moment, the "voice" might find someone else to write her story.

Needless to say, I turned on the light, picked up a pen and a pad of paper and began to write the story of Louisa May "Wildflower" McAllister. It took days and weeks of listening to her and seeing the scenes of her life play out in my imagination. Then it took years of revising and revisiting the story to polish it and get it ready. Not to mention the tremendous amount of faith I had to generate to keep going all those years—faith in myself as a writer and faith in Wildflower's story.

Do ideas always come in this way? No. Sometimes I want to explore a particular theme or a particular place and I lead the storytelling process. But in this instance, it seemed the story led me. My job was to follow and then rewrite to get it as polished as possible.

With that in mind, keep your eyes open for whatever inspires you or creates a spark in your imagination.

It could be a photograph that resonates with you, or a line in a poem or a book that you can't seem to forget.

It could be a scene that you witnessed.

Or an experience that holds a lot of energy for you.

Even a dream can inspire if it is an especially powerful dream.

All are sustenance for a writer in search of a story to tell.

Search Out Beautiful Writing

My advice to aspiring writers is to search out beautiful writing in everything you read. And if you find it, savor it, write it down and study it. Discover what makes it beautiful to you. Then imitate it using your own words.

Here is something I came across recently that was beautiful to me:

"Like any child, I slid into myself perfectly fitted, as a diver meets her reflection in a pool. Her fingertips enter the fingertips on the water, her wrists slide up her arms. The diver wraps herself in her reflection wholly, sealing it at the toes, and wears it as she climbs rising from the pool, and ever after."
--Annie Dillard, author of Pilgrim at Tinker Creek

For me, the metaphor of the diver is a rich visual image. Images help our writing come alive and we can almost feel the water on our own skin. **Beautiful writing is writing that is alive!**

Girl with a Pearl Earring

What interests you?

According to one of my favorite sources about writers called The Writer's Almanac, author Tracy Chevalier moved to London after college to stay for six months, but she fell in love with a British man and never left. She started writing historical novels, and her second book, *Girl with a Pearl Earring* (1999), was a huge best seller.

For the book, Chevalier was inspired one day when she was staring at a poster she had bought when she was 19, a copy of Johannes Vermeer's painting Girl With a Pearl Earring. She imagined what life might have been for the young woman who ended up the subject of that painting. She started the book right away, but she was pregnant and she didn't want the book to get lost in her life as a new mother, so she researched and wrote the whole novel in just eight months.

She said:

"Don't write about what you know — write about what you're interested in. Don't write about yourself — you aren't as interesting as you think."

The Art of "Shitty" First Drafts

In *Bird by Bird: Some Instructions on Writing and Life*, bestselling author, Anne Lamott, has a chapter on writing shitty first drafts.

She says:

"All good writers write them. This is how they end up with good second drafts and terrific third drafts. People tend to look at successful writers, writers who are getting their books published and maybe even doing well financially, and think that they sit down at their desks every morning feeling like a million dollars . . . But this is just the fantasy of the uninitiated. I know some very great writers, writers you love who write beautifully and have made a great deal of money, and not one of them sits down routinely feeling wildly enthusiastic and confident. . . .

"For me and most of the other writers I know, writing is not rapturous. In fact, the only way I can get anything written at all is to write really, really shitty first drafts. The first draft is the child's draft, where you let it all pour out and then let it romp all over the place, knowing that no one is going to see it and that you can shape it later. . . . If the kid wants to get into really sentimental, weepy, emotional territory, you let him. Just get it all down on paper, because there may be something great in those six crazy pages that you would never have gotten to by more rational, grown-up means."

I read *Bird by Bird* over a decade ago, and I still think of Anne Lamott's suggestion every time I start to write something new.

What do you think? Have you written a shitty first draft lately? I hope so.

What Writers Can Learn from Coyotes

When I lived in Colorado, I spotted a total of 26 coyotes over the course of the three years I lived there. Some were within Rocky Mountain National Park, others on the outskirts of our suburban neighborhood where we lived in Fort Collins. They were so close we could actually hear them yip at night.

They are beautiful animals known for their cleverness and resiliency. To their credit, they have learned to adapt to an ever more human-populated landscape. Coyotes have been spotted in Central Park in New York City and one reportedly walked into a Quizno's in Chicago. They are masters at adapting to a world that increasingly sees no value in them.

Sometimes I wonder if writers are in the same predicament. At times it feels like we live on the outskirts of society, doing whatever we have to do to survive. We teach creative writing at community colleges, freelance edit other people's manuscripts, and perhaps go on the lecture circuit, when really all we want to do is let our creativity roam wild, and have it be appreciated, protected and valued.

As it is now, writers need to be clever and cunning about whom we share our creations with, especially when they are just starting out and too young to be released into the world.

Predators lurk in writer's groups, in English departments and in publishing houses. Some of them are well-meaning, yet biting in their criticism, inadvertently destroying the vulnerable and the weak. Or perhaps we are guilty of killing off our own babies because they are not good enough or because we are afraid of the criticism we might receive.

Like coyotes, writers must learn to be resilient, cunning and clever. We must keep both eyes open, to avoid the inevitable dangers, as we roam this wild urban landscape. As we continue to cultivate these traits, I hope that we, too, will thrive like the coyotes.

A Lesson from Tina Fey

In the March 14, 2011 issue of *The New Yorker*, comic actor and writer Tina Fey talks about the lessons she learned from working as a writer in late night television (Saturday Night Live) and the things she learned from producer Lorne Michaels. One of these lessons is something that might interest writers, poets, playwrights, artists, composers, and creative types in any medium. That is: *"the show doesn't go on because it's ready; it goes on because it's eleven-thirty."*

She goes on to say:

"This is something Lorne has said often about 'Saturday Night Live,' but it's a great lesson in not being too precious about your writing. You have to try your hardest to be at the top of your game and improve every joke until the last possible second, but then you have to let it go.

"You can't be that kid standing at the top of the waterslide, overthinking it. You have to go down the chute. (And I'm from a generation in which a lot of people died on waterslides, so this was an important lesson for me to learn.) You have to let people see what you wrote. It will never be perfect, but perfect is overrated. Perfect is boring on live television."

So what do you think? Is there something in your writing life that you are overthinking? Are you that kid standing at the top of the waterslide ready to go down the chute?

1% English Breakfast Tea

My first ten years as a writer, I wrote part-time, stealing time between part-time jobs and raising children. From my experience, the biggest challenge to having a writing life is simply **showing up**. You wouldn't think that sitting at the computer or finding a quiet or (even a loud) coffee shop in order to write would be so hard to do. But it is. There are a thousand and one things that want our attention every day.

One of the ways that I have found over the years that helps me **show up** to write day after day is **rituals.** Before I turn on my computer or grab the hard copy of whatever manuscript I'm working on, I make myself a cup of tea, usually English Breakfast or Assam. If I am at my desk, or at my favorite coffee shop, with a cup of tea brewing I know it's time to start writing. Tea may not be your cup of tea, so to speak. Find something simple that you can do to send a signal to your creative juices that it's time to write.

Another way I've kept writing over the years is to be accountable. I log my writing time, as if it is a job where I will be held accountable. I can look back on this log and know how much time I've put in on a given week and what I've worked on. This also helps me deal with the part of me that chimes in that I'm not doing enough. I have proof in my log that I have shown up.

I have a desire to reach people on a deep level by writing a really good story. I love putting words to the page and that I love seeing where the creative process will take me. I love exploring new settings, new emotions, and new circumstances of my characters.

But I also know myself and the world well enough to know that there are constant roadblocks to fulfilling this desire. So even if it's for ten minutes, create rituals and set time aside in your day to show up to create.

To me, writing is 90% **showing up**, 9% talent, and 1% English Breakfast tea.

101 Excuses Why People Don't Write

Over the last seventeen years, I've attended numerous writers' workshops, groups and conferences, as well as taught classes and given workshops of my own. I've heard lots of excuses about why people don't write. Some of them I've even heard coming from myself! For fun, I came up with a list of 101 excuses why people don't write that book they say they are always going to write. Are any familiar?

1. No one will want to read it anyway
2. I'm not good enough
3. I don't have time to be creative
4. I have to take care of everybody else first
5. I'm just too busy to go on book tours
6. The sun is in my eyes
7. Starbucks has run out of coffee
8. I don't know what to write about
9. No one will understand me
10. I don't think I can handle success
11. I don't think I can handle failure
12. If my parents had encouraged/would encourage me more, I could do this

13. If my spouse/children/teachers/friends would encourage me more, I could do this
14. Writers are navel-gazers
15. I like money too much to become a starving artist
16. It takes too long to learn to write well
17. I don't like criticism
18. There's a ballgame on
19. I don't like to read
20. My twitter followers need me to tweet about what I had for lunch
21. See #1 on the list (it's worth repeating)
22. The spell-check on my computer is set to British English
23. I don't want to have to promote my own book
24. I don't really have anything to say
25. Everybody says I should write a book, but I don't believe them
26. See # 7
27. I want to save on electricity
28. I can't find the pencil sharpener I used in 3rd grade
29. The back of this envelope isn't big enough
30. I can't afford the gasoline to drive to Starbucks
31. There are no comfortable chairs in my house
32. It's too cold
33. It's too hot
34. My facebook friends need me to post something every 5 minutes

35. I work full-time
36. I'm already better than all those bozos writing today
37. If I can't have fame and fortune, I don't want to bother
38. Writing is the get-rich-slow-or-not-at-all plan
39. 99% of all writers get their work rejected by publishers
40. I'll do it when I have more time to devote to it
41. I'll do it when the kids are grown
42. I'll do it after my divorce is final
43. I'll do it after I am independently wealthy
44. I'll do it after I get everything finished with the house
45. I'll do it after everybody I want to write about is dead
46. I need my down time
47. Most of the writer's I know are mentally unbalanced
48. I'm too tired
49. My neighbors are too loud
50. Is that a dog barking?
51. I need to go out to get a drink with my neighbors
52. I have a cut on my finger
53. My back hurts
54. My ghostwriter has disappeared
55. Sarah Palin has already said it all
56. John Grisham doesn't answer my emails
57. Oprah's show has ended, so my book won't be a

book club pick
58. I don't have anything to wear to the Academy Awards
59. My cat won't get off my lap
60. Repeat # 6
61. I need to wash my car
62. Somebody's got to make a living
63. The coffee shop doesn't carry my brand of tea
64. My writer's group is full of critics
65. Writer's conferences are a racket
66. I have a cramp in my big toe
67. It's that time of the month
68. My bowling team will think I'm a sissy
69. I won't have anyone to sit next to at the National Book Awards
70. I'm shy
71. I need to make a list of excuses for my readers so maybe they'll laugh and maybe even buy my books
72. I can't afford to live in New York City where all the famous writers live
73. I don't have time to find an agent
74. Creativity is over-rated
75. I'm sleep-deprived
76. Hemingway killed himself
77. I don't have enough self-esteem
78. I'm a woman
79. I'm a man

80. I'm not white
81. I'm not a person of color
82. I'm thirsty
83. Time to eat
84. I need to see who wins American Idol
85. I secretly find myself boring and have absolutely nothing to say
86. Virginia Woolf drowned herself
87. I don't want to become an alcoholic
88. I don't want to give up drinking
89. I'm much better than a lot of writers out there; they'll be jealous
90. I don't like competition
91. The publishing companies only want stories about vampires
92. No one is getting published these days
93. I ran out of my medication
94. If I had had a better childhood, I could do this
95. My therapist is on vacation for the next two months
96. I have to write the next great American novel
97. I've never read a great American novel
98. See # 83 and repeat
99. I don't like writers
100. Is there an app for this?

Now add your own number one excuse for not writing that book, poem, article, screenplay, or other creative endeavor:

101. _____

Are there any excuses from the list that you particularly resonate with? We all make excuses. But let's face it, excuses are boring, and my guess is that you really do have something to say. So why don't we collectively bury all those excuses in a box in our backyards and get on with it, shall we?

Famous First Lines

Many great things have started with a single line, a single thought. For instance, one day, while grading exams, J.R.R. Tolkien discovered that a student had left one whole page in his examination booklet blank. Tolkien, for reasons unknown even to him, wrote on the page, **"In a hole in the ground there lived a hobbit."**

This single line turned into a bedtime story that he told his children, and from there, a book: *The Hobbit* (1937).

Other powerful first lines in novels:

"Mrs. Dalloway said she would buy the flowers herself."
– Virginia Woolf, *Mrs. Dalloway* (1925)

"Call me Ishmael." – Herman Melville, *Moby-Dick* (1851)

"Many years later, as he faced the firing squad, Colonel Aureliano Buendía was to remember that distant afternoon when his father took him to discover ice."

– Gabriel García Márquez, *One Hundred Years of Solitude* (1967)

"Happy families are all alike; every unhappy family is unhappy in its own way." – Leo Tolstoy, *Anna Karenina* (1877)

"It is a truth universally acknowledged that a single man in possession of a good fortune must be in want of a wife."
– Jane Austen, *Pride and Prejudice* (1813)

"He was an old man who fished alone in a skiff in the Gulf Stream and he had gone eighty-four days now without taking a fish."
– Ernest Hemingway, *The Old Man and the Sea* (1952)

"Ships at a distance have every man's wish on board."
– Zora Neale Hurston, *Their Eyes Were Watching God* (1937)

"They shoot the white girl first."
– Toni Morrison, *Paradise* (1998)

Do you have a favorite first line?

How to Make your Life a Work of Art

Lately I've been focusing on making my life a work of art, which is obviously a big concept to wrap one's mind and life around. But I like a good challenge. Then serendipitously, I found this quote from Virginia Woolf's unfinished memoir "A Sketch of the Past," begun in 1939:

"Perhaps this is the strongest pleasure known to me. It is the rapture I get when in writing I seem to be discovering what belongs to what; making a scene come right; making a character come together. From this I reach what I might call a philosophy; at any rate it is a constant idea of mine; that behind the cotton wool [of daily life] is hidden a pattern; that we--I mean all human beings--are connected with this; that the whole world is a work of art; that we are parts of the work of art. Hamlet or a Beethoven quartet is the truth about this vast mess that we call the world. But there is no Shakespeare, there is no Beethoven . . . we are the words; we are the music; we are the thing itself."

How does this sound to you? Do you think that it's possible that we could all be parts of a work of art?

Art is Work

Ursula K. Le Guin is a successful American author of novels, books for children, and short stories, mainly in the genres of fantasy and science fiction. An interviewer once asked her advice for writers, and she replied:

"I am going to be rather hard-nosed and say that if you have to find devices to coax yourself to stay focused on writing, perhaps you should not be writing what you're writing. And if this lack of motivation is a constant problem, perhaps writing is not your forte. I mean, what is the problem? If writing bores you, that is pretty fatal. If that is not the case, but you find that it is hard going and it just doesn't flow, well, what did you expect? It is work; art is work."

Get to work, dear writer. Create your art!

The Magic of Fiction

In a letter to *The New Yorker*, Michael Cunningham, author of *The Hours*, said:

"Fiction involves trace elements of magic; it works for reasons we can explain and also for reasons we can't. If novels or short-story collections could be weighed strictly in terms of their components (fully developed characters, check; original voice, check; solidly crafted structure, check; serious theme, check) they might satisfy, but they would fail to enchant. A great work of fiction involves a certain frisson that occurs when its various components cohere and then ignite."

I like the idea that fiction has trace elements of magic. I experience this when I read a really good story that captivates me to the point that I don't want to put it down. Another way I know that I am experiencing something very special is that I will purposely slow down my reading so I can savor every word.

May we all create something that the reader and audience finds magical.

Flannery's Secret to Becoming a Great Writer

Southern fiction writer, Flannery O'Connor, spent much of her life on her family farm in Milledgeville, Georgia, raising poultry and writing novels and short stories: *Wise Blood* (1952), *The Violent Bear It Away* (1960), *A Good Man Is Hard to Find* (1955), and *Everything That Rises Must Converge* (1965). This last book of short stories was published after her death in 1964, at the age of 39, from complications of lupus.

She said:

"Everywhere I go I'm asked if I think the university stifles writers. My opinion is that they don't stifle enough of them. There's many a best-seller that could have been prevented by a good teacher."

She also said:

"You shall know the truth, and the truth shall make you odd."

When she was five years old, she trained a chicken to walk backward, and a newsreel company came to her house to make a film about it, which was shown all over the country.

Her comment in the film:

"I was just there to assist the chicken but it was the high point in my life. Everything since has been anticlimax."

So that, my friends, is the secret to becoming a great writer: teach a chicken to walk backward! Success naturally follows.

Poets Talk Poetry

Not everyone gets into poetry. I think a lot of us were tortured as school children with poems that made no sense given the world we lived in. But if we find a poet that speaks a language we can understand, it can help us make sense of the world and give us hope for the creative soul of the world. We must search for the voices that bolster us. That, in turn, will make us better writers.

Here are some thoughts on poetry by poets:

"I don't think poetry is based just on poetry; it is based on a thoroughly lived life. And so I couldn't just decide I was going to write no matter what; I first had to find out what it means to live."
– Jane Hirschfield

"I have always begun with dancing, heard singing, and it always goes back to rhythm. The poems have always started that way. The rhythm, or the beat, even drives the image…My contention is that music, poetry, and dance came into the world together. Civilization in the form of the printing press forced them apart." – Joy Harjo

"No one is a great poet because she is a miserable drunk. No one is a great poet because he has had a nervous breakdown. Suffering, however, can be experienced as a curse or a blessing; the luckiest is the one who can experience it as a blessing." – Carolyn Forché

"Above all, the listener should be able to understand the poem or the song, not be forced to unravel a complicated, self-indulgent puzzle. Offer your art up to the whole world, not just an elite few."
– Lucinda Williams

"Sometimes there is a force of life like the spring which mysteriously takes shape without your even having asked it to take shape, and this is frightening, it is terribly frightening. … Being a poet sometimes puts you at the mercy of life, and life is not always merciful." – James Wright

"I've always been obsessed by the voices that are not normally heard. I think it comes from the women I knew as a child, the women in the kitchen who told the best stories. They knew how the world worked, about human nature, and they were wise, are wise." – Rita Dove

"I believe that poetry, like no other art, articulates an essential part of the human consciousness." – Dana Gioia

"Poets are like steam valves, where the ordinary feelings of ordinary people can escape and be shown." – Sharon Olds

"If there were no poetry on any day in the world, poetry would be invented that day. For there would be an intolerable hunger."
– Muriel Rukeyser

"You choose to be a novelist, but you're chosen to be a poet. This is a gift and it's a tremendous responsibility. You have to be willing to give something terribly intimate and secret of yourself to the world and not care, because you have to believe that what you have to say is important enough." – May Sarton

"To me the world of poetry is a house with thousands of glittering windows. Our words and images, land to land, era to era, shed light on one another. Our words dissolve the shadows we imagine fall between."
– Naomi Shihab Nye

"Poetry keeps longing alive." – Robert Bly

Loneliness

John Steinbeck, author of the Pulitzer Prize-winning *The Grapes of Wrath (1939)*, said:

"A writer out of loneliness is trying to communicate like a distant star sending signals. He isn't telling or teaching or ordering. Rather he seeks to establish a relationship of meaning, of feeling, of observing. We are lonesome animals. We spend all our life trying to be less lonesome."

I'd like to think a writer's life is much less lonely these days. Because of the far reach of the internet, I have writer friends all over the world. Not to mention a wonderful local writer's group that I attend on a regular basis. So I don't often feel lonely.

On the other hand, I can relate to *"trying to communicate like a distant star sending signals."* Part of the business of being a professional writer, in this modern era, is that I am charged with the responsibility of looking for readers who can resonate with my work or hope they find me. So it does feel like I am a distant star sometimes, sending out my signals.

What about you? Can you relate to the (sometimes) loneliness of living a creative life?

Hug A Writer Day

Today I am pretending that I am Master of the Universe (mwa-ha-ha-ha-ha) and am exercising my power to proclaim today as official *Hug A Writer Day*.

Writers don't always know they're appreciated as they struggle to get words on the page. Especially since writing is such a solitary endeavor (most of us are introverts) and we don't always hear that we're doing a good job or that our job is valued at all.

Those who honestly toil at the craft of writing need to know that you value their writing efforts, whether you like their writing or not, whether you have even read something they have written. An advanced, cultured and humane society needs its writers.

So tell your spouse or a friend that it's *Hug a Writer Day* and soak in their appreciative embrace.

An Essentially Private Business

When William Wall—Irish novelist, poet and short-story writer—was asked why the bio on his homepage was so brief (only 25 words), he responded:

"I don't believe that the details of my life have any relevance to a reading of my work. Besides, in many ways I lead a pretty boring life — I get up early and work as much as I can, I make coffee etc. What I want to say about my life, my thinking and my beliefs is in my books and other published materials. If I wanted to be a 'celebrity' (whatever the hell that is), whose every living moment is of vital interest to 'the public,' I wouldn't be a writer. Writing is an essentially private business. I'd even go so far as to say that it's an intimate one."

By the way, here is the 25 word bio on his homepage:

Born in Cork 1955
Grew up in the coastal village of Whitegate
Educated at University College Cork
Degree in Philosophy & English
Married. Two sons.

I go back and forth on this issue. As not only a writer, but an avid reader, I like to Google my favorite authors and see what they're up to. Sometimes reading a review, interview or a blog post by or about them makes me want to buy another of their books. But as a shy kid, who grew up to be an introverted writer, I am always challenged by putting a lot of information out there. Yet, I still do it.

What do you think? Do you like knowing the personal details of the writers you read?

My website bio is at least 500 words, maybe more. Could you do your own bio in 25 words?

Here's the one I came up with:

Born next to third oldest river in the world.
Loves to laugh.
Into symbolism, trees, wildlife, my family, intuition.
Writer of courageous and transformational stories.

Writers Who Are Also Mothers

Writer Louise Erdrich said:

> "By having children, I've both sabotaged and saved myself as a writer. [...] With a child you certainly can't be a Bruce Chatwin or a Hemingway, living the adventurer-writer life. No running with the bulls at Pamplona. If you value your relationships with your children, you can't write about them. You have to make up other, less convincing children. There is also one's inclination to be charming instead of presenting a grittier truth about the world. But then, having children has also made me this particular writer. Without my children, I'd have written with less fervor; I wouldn't understand life in the same way. I'd write fewer comic scenes, which are the most challenging. I'd probably have become obsessively self-absorbed, or slacked off. Maybe I'd have become an alcoholic. Many of the writers I love most were alcoholics. I've made my choice, I sometimes think: Wonderful children instead of hard liquor."

As for me, I have two amazing daughters who are launched into the world at this point, but when I started writing they were still in middle school and high school. As a single parent, I had to fit writing in where I could. I held down part-time jobs and wrote at four in the morning. I wrote after they went to bed. I wrote in the car while waiting on Violin lessons and band practices.

I'd like to think writing actually made me a better mom because—then, as now—I feel at my most authentic when I write. And isn't modeling genuineness and authenticity perhaps a parent's most aspiring goal?

A Pulitzer in Bubble Wrap?

According to Writer's Almanac, Jhumpa Lahiri had no idea that her first novel, *The Interpreter of Maladies*, was a contender for any prizes, and then one day she got a phone call. She said:

"I was in my apartment. We had just come back from a short trip to Boston and I was heating up some soup for my lunch. My suitcases were still not unpacked. And the phone rang. It was one or two in the afternoon. The person who called me was from Houghton Mifflin, my publisher, but no one I knew, and she said, 'I need to know what year you were born.' And then she asked some other fact like where I was born. I just told her. Sometimes people need some information for a reading, for a flyer or something. And then she said, 'You don't know why I am calling, do you?' And I said, 'No, why are you calling?' And she said, 'You just won the Pulitzer.' "

It was the first time a paperback had ever won the Pulitzer. *The Interpreter of Maladies* became an immediate best seller. Lahiri was uncomfortable with her new fame — she said:

"If I stop to think about fans, or best-selling, or not best-selling, or good reviews, or not-good reviews, it just becomes too much. It's like staring at the mirror all day."

So she doesn't read reviews and she keeps her Pulitzer wrapped in bubble wrap. I think there may be wisdom in that.

What would you do if you won a big award? Would you keep your Pulitzer in bubble wrap?

Writing Later In Life

Elizabeth Gilbert, author of the mega-bestselling memoir *Eat, Pray, Love,* has encouraging words for people who come to writing later in life. She says:

> *"Writing is not like dancing or modeling; it's not something where — if you missed it by age 19 — you're finished. It's never too late. Your writing will only get better as you get older and wiser. If you write something beautiful and important, and the right person somehow discovers it, they will clear room for you on the bookshelves of the world — at any age. At least try."*

I can second that. I didn't start writing until I was nearly 40. I was a psychotherapist with a full private practice and had the realization that if I died at that moment, a lot of people might come to my funeral, but I would die having never done what I was called to do, which was to write.

I agree that it's never too late to claim your "voice," in whatever arena you feel you have things to say. It doesn't matter if you're a late bloomer, as long as you bloom!

The Courage to Follow Your Heart and Intuition

"Your time is limited, so don't waste it living someone else's life... Don't let the noise of others' opinions drown out your own inner voice. And most important, have the courage to follow your heart and intuition. They somehow already know what you truly want to become. Everything else is secondary."
– Steve Jobs, co-founder of Apple computers

Are there people or situations in your life that are drowning out your inner voice? As you know, this can be devastating for writers and creative types. Are you willing to do what Steve Jobs suggests? Do you have the courage to follow your heart and intuition? If not yet, keep reading.

Kill Your Darlings

William Faulkner is rumored to have coined the literary expression "kill your darlings," but the expression appears to originate with British author Sir Arthur Quiller-Couch.

When describing "style" in his 1916 publication "On the Art of Writing," Couch says that "style" is something which "is not—can never be—extraneous ornament." In an effort to stay on course, he created a practical rule to follow:

"Whenever you feel an impulse to perpetrate a piece of exceptionally fine writing, obey it—whole-heartedly—and delete it before sending your manuscript to press. Murder your darlings."

"Murder your darlings" has since become "kill your darlings" as attributed to William Faulkner who is famously quoted to have said, *"In writing, you must kill all your darlings."*

Bestselling author Stephen King is a big advocate of the "kill your darlings" approach, and discusses it in his book "On Writing," published in 2000. King advises:

"Mostly when I think of pacing, I go back to Elmore Leonard, who explained it so perfectly by saying he just left out the boring parts. This suggest cutting to speed the pace, and that's what most of us end up having

to do (kill your darlings, kill your darlings, even when it breaks your egocentric little scribbler's heart, kill your darlings)...I got a scribbled comment that changed the way I rewrote my fiction once and forever. Jotted below the machine-generated signature of the editor was this note: 'Not bad, but PUFFY. You need to revise for length. Formula: 2nd Draft = 1st Draft − 10%. Good luck.'"

How about a poet's take on the same topic? See what you think of Jane Hirshfield's poem, *Character and Life* (from *After*, 2006, HarperCollins):

The young novelist held underwater
the head of the character in his book he loved best.
In the book, and as he wrote,
he counted until he was sure it was finished.

So are you willing to "kill your darlings" in order to make your writing stronger and save boredom for your reader? Or are there things in your non-writing life that you need to get rid of but are hanging onto for sentimental reasons?

Encouraging Quotes about Writing and the Creative Life

"What a writer can do, what a fiction writer or a poet or an essay writer can do, is re-engage people with their own humanity. Fiction and essays can create empathy for the theoretical stranger."
– Barbara Kingsolver

"There's room for everybody on the planet to be creative and conscious if you are your own person. If you're trying to be like somebody else, then there isn't." – Tori Amos

Everyone deserves Sanctuary a place to go where you are safe
Art offers Sanctuary to everyone willing
to open their hearts as well as their eyes

– Nikki Giovanni, "Art Sanctuary"
  from *Quilting the Black-Eyed Pea*

"The writer doesn't trust his enemies, of course, who are wrong about his writing, but he doesn't trust his friends, either, who he hopes are right. The writer trusts nothing he writes — it should be too reckless and alive for that, it should be beautiful and menacing and slightly out of his control. It should want to live itself somehow."
– Joy Williams

Julian Barnes said that a great book *"is a book that describes the world in a way that has not been done before; and that is recognized by those who read it as telling new truths — about society or the way in which emotional lives are led, or both."*

"Writing saved me from the sin and inconvenience of violence."
–Alice Walker

"Stories have to be told or they die, and when they die we can't remember who we are or why we are here."
– Sue Monk Kidd, *The Secret Life of Bees*

"When I'm writing, I am concentrating almost wholly on concrete detail: the color a room is painted, the way a drop of water rolls off a wet leaf after a rain." – Donna Tartt

"You have to write the book that wants to be written. And if the book will be too difficult for grown-ups, then you write it for children."
– Madeleine L'Engle

"I have this sense of urgency about what I want to get done and I discipline myself by keeping to myself."
– Marilynne Robinson

Do any of these quotes speak to you? Perhaps write your favorite one down and keep it by the place you write.

Your Writing Routine

Charles Bukowski has published more than 15 wildly popular books of fiction and poetry, including *Run with the Hunted* (1962), and *The Days Run Away Like Wild Horses Over the Hills* (1969).

Late in his life he said:

"Every day I'll wake up around noon. Then I'll go to the track and I'll play the horses ... Then I'll come back and I'll swim and ... have dinner and I'll go upstairs and I'll sit at the computer and I'll crack me a bottle [of wine] and I'll listen to some Mahler or Sibelius and I'll write, with this rhythm, like always."

Needless to say, every writer's process is different. My day doesn't look anything like Charles Bukowski's day. For instance I wake up early, and then I take a walk by the river (most days). Then I am back home to write by about 9 and write until around 12:30. After lunch I do the business of writing—submissions, marketing, typing changes into the computer—and then I fix dinner. I edit other people's manuscripts in the evenings or during the day if I have a deadline.

I don't play the horses or Mahler and if I cracked open a bottle of wine, I would probably fall asleep after one glass. My rhythm is a little different, but that doesn't make it right or wrong, nor is Charles Bukowski's because it seems to have worked for him. We all do what we have to do to get the job done and no schedule is set in stone. (Forgive the clichés.) Sometimes I do things differently just to shake things up and sometimes deadlines blur the lines.

What about you? Do you have a set writing routine or a time when you feel most creative? What does your typical day look like? If you don't have a typical writing day, create one.

Yellow Legal Pads

Maya Angelou, author of *Why the Caged Bird Sings*, still writes on yellow legal pads.
She said:

"I see a yellow pad, and my knees get weak, and I salivate."

According to Wikipedia, Angelou has used the same "writing ritual" for many years. She would wake early in the morning and check into a hotel room, where the staff was instructed to remove any pictures from the walls. She would write on yellow legal pads while laying on the bed, with only a bottle of sherry, a deck of cards to play solitaire, Roget's Thesaurus, and the Bible, and would leave by the early afternoon.

She would average 10–12 pages of written material a day, which she edited down to three or four pages in the evening.

We all have writing rituals. I would find it hard to write without a cup of tea on my side table or desk. I also have several places around my home that I write depending on the time of year. In the spring and summer I am often outside on my screened in back porch. In winter I'm often in the front room where the sun pours into the house. Other times I'm in a corner of my bedroom in my favorite chair where I can watch birds at the bird feeders. I also have a favorite coffee shop that I sometimes go to if I feel the need to get out of the house, as well as a place where I sit by the river.

How and where do you write? On yellow legal pads or a laptop computer? Do you have a place that you especially like to write?

Storytelling

In *The Atlantic* magazine, travel and fiction writer Paul Theroux talks about the place of fiction in the cultural landscape.

The Atlantic: *How would you characterize the state of fiction today? Are we producing more or fewer good writers than in the past, and more or fewer good readers? How have the writing life and the reading life changed since you were starting out, 40 years ago?*

Paul Theroux: *Fiction writing, and the reading of it, and book buying, have always been the activities of a tiny minority of people, even in the most-literate societies. Herman Melville died in utter obscurity. F. Scott Fitzgerald's books were either out of print or not selling when he died. Paul Bowles was able to live and write (and smoke dope) only because he wrote for Holiday, the great old travel magazine. Nor are writers particularly highly regarded. A few years ago, Boston—a city of writers and thinkers—needed to name a beautiful bridge and a graceful tunnel. The first was named for a recently deceased social worker and civil-rights activist, the second for a baseball player. This happens in most U.S. cities, partly from ingrained philistinism and also from the non-reader's fear of books, of writers in general. Many aspects of the writing life have changed since I published my first book, in the 1960s. It is more corporate, more driven by profits and marketing, and generally less congenial—but my day is the same: get out of bed, procrastinate, sit down at my desk, try to write something.*

I agree with Paul Theroux. Writers stay the same. We get up and face another day of trying to create stories, essays and poetry that we hope will resonate with our readers. Are you writing or creating something today?

Writer's Block, Anyone?

Fran Lebowitz is at work on a novel that was commissioned more than 20 years ago, and publishers are still waiting for it. For one reason or another, a lot of people get stuck when it comes to completing their creative endeavors.

For many, writer's block or creativity block is a very real dilemma. Books and articles are written about it that search for the answers and offer strategies. Theories range from fear of failure to fear of success, perfectionism to procrastination.

Here's what Fran Lebowitz has to say about her chronic writer's block:

"I have a hard time writing. Most writers have a hard time writing. I have a harder time than most because I'm lazier than most. ... I would have made a perfect heiress. I enjoy lounging. And reading. The other problem I have is fear of writing. The act of writing puts you in confrontation with yourself, which is why I think writers assiduously avoid writing."

Writing takes courage. It takes an attitude of fearlessness. Laziness isn't an option. As the saying goes, *what we resist, persists*. Are you willing to step into those writing projects that you've been avoiding?

The Power of Vulnerability

Writers, artists and creative types are some of the most vulnerable people I know. To put yourself out there, to risk criticism about your work and dare to create in a culture that doesn't always value creativity, is hard. But despite this predicament, Brene Brown (a very left brain scientist/social worker/researcher) believes that this vulnerability may hold the key to deep, soulful living.

She gave a 20 minute TED talk on The Power of Vulnerability that I think is compelling and courageous for someone in her field. This was part of her appeal for me. Her conclusions are something you would expect from artists and poets, not people who come to the conclusion through documented, left-brained research.

She says on her website:

"When I stand back and look at the work I've done over the past ten years, I can clearly see that the heart of my work is about the very human need to live with authenticity, love and belonging, and a resilient spirit. I call this WholeHearted living. I have dedicated my career to studying difficult topics like shame, empathy, and vulnerability because I want to know, in my head and in my heart, why we're all so afraid to let

our true selves be seen and known. I want to hear and tell the stories that inspire us to be real, imperfect, and powerful. The core of WholeHearted living is connection."

And then later:

"I recently wrote a piece on my blog about my journey to live authentically and soulfully. I received several emails asking me what I meant by living authentically and soulfully. For me, the soulful piece is about living in the spirited space that connects my head and my heart (which is a huge challenge for a head person, like me). Trying to come up with a definition for authenticity forced me to tap deep into my research to find the words that capture what I've learned in my work and reflects what I've actually lived."

She also said:

"Owning our story can be hard but not nearly as difficult as spending our lives running from it. Embracing our vulnerabilities is risky but not nearly as dangerous as giving up on love and belonging and joy—the experiences that make us the most vulnerable. Only when we are brave enough to explore the darkness will we discover the infinite power of our light."

What about you? Would your life look any differently if you chose to live it authentically and soulfully? How would this affect your writing, art, and creativity? As far as I'm concerned, writers are the perfect candidates for *WholeHearted Living*. In fact, I think it may be part of our job description.

Rejection and Perseverance

According to Writer's Almanac, Canadian children's writer, L.M. Montgomery, was born on Prince Edward Island in 1874. Her mother died when she was very young and her father sent her to live with her mother's parents. There were no other children around, just Lucy and her grandparents, and she spent a lot of time reading and writing poems. She left home for a few years to teach, but when her grandfather died, she came home to live with her grandmother, and she stayed with her for the next 13 years.

During that time, she wrote her first novel, about an orphan girl with bright red hair who gets sent to live with a couple from Prince Edward Island who were hoping for a boy instead of a girl.

The manuscript got rejected over and over, so she put it away in a hatbox and turned to other things. But eventually, she got it back out, read it, decided it wasn't that bad after all, and sent it out again.

This time it got accepted, and in 1908, *Anne of Green Gables* was published and became a classic children's book. Since its publication, *Anne of Green Gables* has sold more than 50 million books. In addition, this book is taught to students around the world and has been captured on film many times.

When my daughters were young they read all the *Anne of Green Gables* books and we would have weekend marathons of watching the CBC mini-series by the same name.

What if Lucy Maud Montgomery had left her stories in her hatbox?

Some stories (or poems or essays) need to be out into the world so they can work their magic. They need your perseverance. They need your dedication and belief.

What manuscripts do you have in a "hatbox" that you may need to get out again and resubmit or publish yourself? What do you need to create that you haven't yet? Perhaps the time is now!

Top 10 New Year's Resolutions for Writers

Last year, to celebrate the New Year, I created what I believe to be the Top 10 New Year's Resolutions for writers, artists and creative types. See what you think.

1) Create—practice your craft—every day.

2) Believe in yourself as a writer and an artist. If you're not there yet, "fake it till you make it."

3) Suspend judgment on whether or not you "should" be writing and allow yourself to be otherwise creative. Avoid people who have the same judgment.

4) Cultivate resilience by writing and submitting twice as much as you have in the past.

5) Give random acts of encouragement to other writers, artists, and other creative types.

6) Be grateful for every minute you find to create.

7) Celebrate your courage and perseverance as you strive to get your work out into the world.

8) Support the arts locally and globally: buy books, attend concerts and plays, frequent galleries, buy original art, etc.

9) Experience beauty every day.

10) Send your inner critic on an extended holiday.

Can you think of other resolutions that you'd like to add? Which of these resolutions are you willing to commit to for the next twelve months?

Avoid Success at all Costs?

I love Scott London's interviews and recently found one of his most popular blog posts called "Avoid Success at all Costs." In a world that tells us that we must be either best-selling authors or nothing, this was refreshing to read.

In it he says:

"The fierce drive to accomplish something and make a name for ourselves too often takes us down the wrong path. In the end, the qualities we're looking for are those that go with being free of worldly success.

"Ultimately, the aim must be to become indifferent to what people think of us — to become immune to applause and unmoved by criticism. There is integrity in that.

The goal must be to be present with what we're doing — so present that we do it gracefully, effortlessly. There is great joy in that."

He goes on to say that success tends to be short-lived when it does come and that we all have to face ourselves again sooner or later.

"When that day arrives," he says, *"we have no choice but to find something more lasting to pin our hopes to."* And to Scott London, success ultimately leads to another path of service.

Do you think there is integrity in being immune to what other people think of us? How might your success be another path to service?

12 Quotes by Poets about Poetry

"Poetry is the art of creating imaginary gardens with real toads."
– Marianne Moore

"Poetry is the rhythmic, inevitably narrative, movement from an over-clothed blindness to a naked vision that depends in its intensity on the strength of the labour put into the creation of the poetry. My poetry is, or should be, useful to me for one reason: it is the record of my individual struggle from darkness towards some measure of light."
– Dylan Thomas

"I'm not very good at praying, but what I experience when I'm writing a poem is close to prayer. I feel it in different degrees and not with every poem. But in certain ways writing is a form of prayer."
– Denise Levertov

"Poetry is what makes me laugh or cry or yawn, what makes my toenails twinkle, what makes me want to do this or that or nothing."
– Dylan Thomas

"Poetry is the journal of the sea animal living on land, wanting to fly in the air. Poetry is a search for syllables to shoot at the barriers of the unknown and the unknowable. Poetry is a phantom script telling how rainbows are made and why they go away." – Carl Sandburg

"If I were in solitary confinement, I'd never write another novel, and probably not keep a journal, but I'd write poetry, because poems, you see, are between God and me." – May Sarton

"Every day I walk out into the world / to be dazzled, then to be reflective." – Mary Oliver

"There's no money in poetry, but then there's no poetry in money, either." – Robert Graves

To see the Summer Sky
Is Poetry, though never in a Book it lie -
True Poems flee.

– Emily Dickinson

"One must think like a hero to behave like a merely decent human being." – May Sarton

"Poetry is life distilled." – Gwendolyn Brooks

"Poets are like magicians, searching for magical phrases to pull rabbits out of people's souls."
– Terri Guillemets

Do you have a favorite quote or a favorite poet? Reading poetry can make us better prose writers. No kidding. Try it.

Writing Elf Exposed

Early in her career, Anne Tyler—author of *The Accidental Tourist* (1985), *Back When We Were Grownups* (2001), and *Digging to America* (2006)—decided she did not want to be a public person, so she stopped giving readings and only does occasional written interviews.

She said:

"Any time I talk in public about writing, I end up not able to do any writing. It's as if some capricious Writing Elf goes into a little sulk whenever I expose him."

A lot of writers, like me, are introverts. Book signings and public appearances are the last thing we want to do. But we also want to find readers and help readers find us.

Perhaps the internet is the solution for introverted writers, poets, artists, et al. If you would opt out of public appearances where you talk about your craft to avoid the sulking "writing elf," don't worry! You don't need to have a big public persona to write. In fact, you could lose a lot of precious energy thinking about this in the early stages of being a writer. Your first priority is to learn the craft and write a really great story.

The Most Difficult Job You Will Ever Have

In an Op-Ed piece in *The New York Times* entitled "Boxers, Briefs and Books," John Grisham talks about how he became a writer. Here is an excerpt:

"*Writing was not a childhood dream of mine. I do not recall longing to write as a student. I wasn't sure how to start. Over the following weeks I refined my plot outline and fleshed out my characters. One night I wrote 'Chapter One' at the top of the first page of a legal pad; the novel, 'A Time to Kill,' was finished three years later.*

"*The book didn't sell, and I stuck with my day job, defending criminals, preparing wills and deeds and contracts. Still, something about writing made me spend large hours of my free time at my desk.*

"*I had never worked so hard in my life, nor imagined that writing could be such an effort. It was more difficult than laying asphalt, and at times more frustrating than selling underwear. But it paid off. Eventually, I was able to leave the law and quit politics. Writing's still the most difficult job I've ever had — but it's worth it.*"

So what do you think? Is writing the most difficult job you've ever had? In many ways it has been for me. There are very few jobs where I've had to deal with so much ongoing rejection. It is endless. And the acceptances were few and far between in the last seventeen years. That's why you have to really love it. You have to believe that it's the only thing that will give your life meaning. This sounds extreme, perhaps, but if dedication and determination aren't something you're willing to develop, you might want to do something easier.

Revising Is About Re-visioning

Not long ago, our house was basically a construction zone. We had these changes planned for months; we geared up for the disruption it would inevitably cause; we vowed to rise above the chaos and stay focused on the finished product.

When we were in the thick of it, we resorted to living a life of clichés. "Take it one day at a time," we told each other. "Keep your eye on the prize," we gently reminded ourselves. "Stay steady," we said seriously, when it felt like the "wheels were coming off" the rickety go-cart of our sanity.

At the same time that our house was being taken over by noise and very helpful, wonderful tradesmen, I had been seeking out quieter locations to work on the revisions to my new novel. As nail guns secured oak flooring where worn out carpet used to be, I hammered away at every scene, every paragraph, and every word trying to create something new, fresh, and vital.

Revising is about Re-visioning.

Before the construction started, we re-visioned our house, wanting to update it to fit our aesthetics and our lifestyle.

As I re-visioned every scene and character in my manuscript, I moved sections of text around, enhanced or expanded a scene, as well as took a hard look at anything that slowed down the pacing and effectiveness of the novel. I did this because for me, the goal was and is always to write a really good story – a story that will keep readers interested and engaged and have them remembering the characters long after they have finished reading the book.

To this end, revising (also known as rewriting) can be subtle, removing a word here or there, adding a different metaphor, expanding dialogue or description. At other times, revising can contain moments of complete demolition. Much of revising, or re-visioning, is about getting rid of anything (characters, scenes, extra words) that doesn't serve the story, just like a home renovation is getting rid of anything that doesn't serve the ultimate layout or vision a person has for their home. But it's also about building: creating richer, more compelling characters, taking more risks and perhaps expanding the scenes that work.

Revising is about being able to hold the tension of the chaos that occurs before a creation is complete. In the end, whether you're revising your book, your home, your work, your relationship or some other aspect of your life, for me it's about creating a work of art.

May we all take each day one day at a time, keep our eye on the prize and, by all means, stay steady. Hopefully, staying steady means you are writing consistently. That would be really good news.

Finding the Best Titles

On the fiftieth anniversary of Harper Lee's only novel, *To Kill a Mockingbird,* I found myself pondering the title.

The story is narrated by six-year-old Scout Finch in the fictional town of Maycomb, Alabama. It was an immediate best-seller, a Pulitzer Prize winner, and an instant American classic. Many people believe it to be one of the greatest works of southern fiction ever written. It continues to sell incredibly well, with 30 million copies still in print.

The book's title appears in a scene in chapter 10, where Scout remembers something her dad, Atticus, has said and asks her neighbor Miss Maudie about it.

"I'd rather you shot at tin cans in the back yard, but I know you'll go after birds. Shoot all the blue jays you want, if you can hit 'em, but remember it's a sin to kill a mockingbird."

That was the only time I ever heard Atticus say it was a sin to do something, and I asked Miss Maudie about it.

"Your father's right," she said. "Mockingbirds don't do one thing but make music for us to enjoy. They don't eat up people's gardens, don't nest in corncribs, they don't do one thing but sing their hearts out for us. That's why it's a sin to kill a mockingbird."

For years after seeing the movie as a girl, I wished that Atticus Finch was my father, since my personal father wasn't quite up for the task. And like millions of other kids in the States, I was required to read *To Kill a Mockingbird* in high school. But I didn't understand this book's power until I re-read it a few years ago.

Do you ever have trouble coming up with the titles of your books or essays? Sometimes the best way to find one is to pull it from the book itself. It may be hidden away in a phrase or buried within a page of the book like treasure waiting to be unearthed.

How to Write in 700 Easy Lessons

While reading the Atlantic Monthly 2010 Fiction Issue, I came across an essay by Richard Bausch entitled: "How to Write in 700 Easy Lessons: The Case Against Writing Manuals."

If you are a professional writer, or aspire to be one, you might find it interesting. When I was starting out, I read my share of books on the "how to" of writing, but I ultimately found that I learned how to write by doing the actual work of writing every day and by reading a lot of literary fiction (the genre I write most in).

Here is an excerpt from the article that I highlighted when I read it:

"Finally, a word about this kind of instruction: it is always less effective than actually reading the books of the writers who precede you, and who are contemporary with you.

"There are too many 'how-to' books on the market, and too many would-be writers are reading these books in the mistaken idea that this will teach them to write. I never read such a book in my life, and I never will. What I know about writing I know from having read the work of the great writers. If you really want to learn how to write, do that. Read Shakespeare, and all the others whose work has withstood time and circumstance and changing fashions and the assaults of the ignorant and the

bigoted; read those writers and don't spend a lot of time analyzing them. Digest them, swallow them all, one after another, and try to sound like them for a time.

"Learn to be as faithful to the art and craft as they all were, and follow their example. That is, wide reading and hard work. One doesn't write out of some intellectual plan or strategy; one writes from a kind of beautiful necessity born of the reading of thousands of good stories, poems, plays… One is deeply involved in literature, and thinks more of writing than of being a writer. It is not a stance."

I have found that most advice from professional writers affirms that reading helps people become better writers.

Deep Conversations

Would you be happier if you spent more time discussing creativity and the meaning of life — and less time talking about the weather? According to a blog post at the *New York Times* called "Talk Deeply, Be Happy," a study has shown that deep conversations make people happier than small talk.

As a lover of deep conversations, I am fortunate enough to have some really good friends, as well as a mate with whom I have talks with depth quite frequently. I realize what a blessing this is.

I would even go so far as to say that a good novel, good non-fiction, or a good poem is a deep conversation between the writer and the reader.

Here's what Matthias Mehl says about the findings:

"It may sound counter-intuitive, but people who spend more of their day having deep discussions and less time engaging in small talk seem to be happier," said Matthias Mehl, a psychologist at the University of Arizona who published the study.

"We found this so interesting, because it could have gone the other way — it could have been, 'Don't worry, be happy' — as long as you

surf on the shallow level of life you're happy, and if you go into the existential depths you'll be unhappy," Dr. Mehl said.

But, he proposed, substantive conversation seemed to hold the key to happiness for two main reasons: both because human beings are driven to find and create meaning in their lives, and because we are social animals who want and need to connect with other people.

"By engaging in meaningful conversations, we manage to impose meaning on an otherwise pretty chaotic world," Dr. Mehl said. *"And interpersonally, as you find this meaning, you bond with your interactive partner, and we know that interpersonal connection and integration is a core fundamental foundation of happiness."*

Are you happiest when you have a deep, meaningful conversation? Talking about creativity, courage and soul is my way of putting something that has deeper meaning out into the world.

Stopping the Divine Dance of Avoidance

According to The Writer's Almanac, Elizabeth George is a woman considered by many to be the greatest living mystery novelist. She graduated from college with a major in English. Rather than sitting down to write novels, which she knew was her calling, she did what she calls the "Divine Dance of Avoidance."

...Meaning she was busy doing everything except writing. She got a teaching credential, became a high school English teacher, and got a master's degree in counseling. Every summer break, when she'd get 10 weeks off of school to write, she would be filled with anxiety about starting a book, about whether her plot or characters would be any good, or whether she'd be able to write convincingly, or whether she'd be able to finish anything she started.

And then, in 1983, her husband bought a computer in order to write his graduate thesis. They'd never owned a computer, only typewriters, and she said she knew it could make her "life as a writer much easier," to be able to cut and paste and edit on the screen. She chose to make it a defining moment.

When the computer arrived at their house, she said:

"I was faced with the simplest life question I've ever had to answer. I asked myself whether, on my deathbed, I wanted to sigh and say, 'I could have written a novel' or 'I wrote a novel.' Believe me, the answer was simplicity itself."

Her first novel was rejected by everyone she sent it to, but along with their rejection, the people at Scribner's said some nice things about her writing style, and she was thoroughly encouraged.

She made a trip to England, wrote a second English crime novel which was similarly rejected, made another trip to England the following summer, and when she returned she had 42 days left until she needed to go back to the classroom to teach high school English for the year. She felt like she'd come up with a great plot, structure, and twist, and she was determined to write the novel before school started up. So she sat down and wrote for 8 to 16 hours a day. She finished the first draft of the novel in three and a half weeks. She revised it and sent it off to an agent. The agent sold it to Bantam Books, which was just beginning a line of hardcover mysteries.

The book was A *Great Deliverance*, her first published title and the first in the Inspector Lynley series, and it was a great success. She quit her high school teaching job of 13 years and began writing full time.

Her writing process:

Elizabeth George writes five days a week when she's working on the first draft, and when she's on subsequent drafts, she writes seven days a week. She always gets up at 6 a.m., she says, feeds the dog and takes vitamins and works out on an Exercycle for 30 minutes while reading a meditation book, then inspirational book, then a novel. And she lifts weights for 35 minutes while watching The Today Show. She meditates for 10 minutes, sits down at her desk, reads great literature for about 15 minutes — something along the lines of Jane Austen — and writes a paragraph or page or two in a journal. And then she begins to work on the novel she's writing. She keeps a plot outline, and every day she writes a minimum of five pages, even if she's on the road for book tours or on vacation.

George said,

"The only way to succeed at the writing life is to be able to live according to a schedule that accommodates time to write."

Keep in mind very few writers are fortunate enough to have this kind of time to write, so don't let this discourage you.

Most of us fit writing in whenever we can in the midst of working, teaching classes, leading workshops or doing professional editing. That doesn't mean that we don't also do the "Divine Dance of Avoidance." What about you? Are you willing to stop the dance?

Don't Look Back!
Wisdom from a Composer

Jennifer Higdon has composer anxiety, but she stuck with it and now she has a Pulitzer Prize for music for her Violin Concerto. In an article in the New York Times, Ms. Higdon said she doesn't experience writer's block and composes fast:

"I think it's a little like working out. You get that muscle going, where you're just using it all the time. So I tend to move on to the next project pretty quickly."

Despite some days of writing anxiety and dark moods, she rarely puts down her pen.

Composing "is a very serious need," Ms. Higdon said. *"I have to express things."*

Many writers could say this, too.

Ms. Higdon has had her share of detractors, who told her she couldn't compose because she had started so late; that a flute performance major couldn't be a composer; that she would never make a living; and that she would never get into graduate school. Some male composers grumbled to her face that her she's only been successful because she's a woman.

"Everyone runs into naysayers," Ms. Higdon said, *"but if you love something enough and feel passionately enough, you just go on ahead, walk right round the person saying it, proceed down the road and don't look back."*

It's true, we all have naysayers. They may be outer critics or inner critics. But it's important to not let them stop us. We must all proceed down the road of our dreams and DON'T LOOK BACK!

Fabulous Quotes about Writing and Creativity

"What is to give light, must endure burning."
– Viktor Frankl, and motto of The Sun magazine

"I grapple with having equal proportions of narcissism and low self-esteem." – Anne Lamott

"Be as a bird perched on a frail branch that she feels bending beneath her, still she sings away all the same, knowing she has wings."
– Victor Hugo

"It's none of their business that you have to learn to write. Let them think you were born that way."
– Ernest Hemingway

"Happiness is when what you think, what you say, and what you do are in harmony." – Mahatma Gandhi

"A room without books is like a body without a soul."
– Marcos Cicero

"Above all, be the heroine of your life. Not the victim."
– Nora Ephron

"All truly great thoughts are conceived while walking."
– Friedrich Nietzsche

"Take rest; a field that has rested gives a bountiful crop."
– Ovid (43 BC - 17 AD)

"What lies behind us and what lies before us, are tiny matters compared to what lies within us."
– Ralph Waldo Emerson

"If you are lucky enough to find a way of life you love, you have to find the courage to live it." – John Irving

"If I were in solitary confinement, I'd never write another novel, and probably not keep a journal, but I'd write poetry, because poems, you see, are between God and me." – May Sarton

"I work continuously within the shadow of failure. For every novel that makes it to my publisher's desk, there are at least five or six that died on the way." – Gail Godwin

"Twenty years from now you will more disappointed by the things that you didn't do than by the ones you did do. So throw off the bowlines. Sail away from the safe harbor. Catch the trade winds in your sails. Explore. Dream. Discover." – Mark Twain

A Choice or Chosen?

Here is a powerful quote from writer, Paul Auster, author of *The New York Trilogy* (1985–86), a set of idiosyncratic detective stories that deal with questions of identity and existential thought, as well as a memoir, *The Invention of Solitude* (1982), and several other books.

He wrote:

"Becoming a writer is not a 'career decision' like becoming a doctor or a policeman. You don't choose it so much as get chosen, and once you accept the fact that you're not fit for anything else, you have to be prepared to walk a long, hard road for the rest of your days."

He also said:

"I don't know why I do what I do. If I did know, I probably wouldn't feel the need to do it. ... Surely it is an odd way to spend your life — sitting alone in a room with a pen in your hand, hour after hour, day after day, year after year, struggling to put words on pieces of paper in order to give birth to what does not exist — except in your head. Why on earth would anyone want to do such a thing? The only answer I have

ever been able to come up with is: because you have to, because you have no choice."

Why on earth would anyone want to do such a hard thing? I ask myself the same question sometimes.

I am 200 pages into the writing of my new novel. If I'm really lucky, I'll have a first draft ready in a few more months. The process of building a story out of my imagination is intense and amazing, as well as exhausting. But building a story from the ground up is only the beginning of the process. To take a book (or work of art, or poem, or song) from inception to publication and beyond, is a journey of a thousand steps. It is the biggest mountain you will ever climb. But wow, what a vista!

Writing (or painting, sculpting, or singing) every day is only part of the training.

Would I choose to do this if I were a sane, reasonable person? That's debatable. I would prefer to do something much easier. Something that didn't involve rejection and criticism. Not to mention, marketing! Yet I keep doing it. Day after day. Year after year.

Despite the hardships which the devotion to an art undoubtedly brings, I keep going. Why? Because if I didn't, I feel like I would lose the best part of myself. The part that is creative, resilient, brave and a believer in imagination and artistic expression. The part that believes in soul.

Something has to keep you going, too. What will it be?

Secretly. Compulsively. Shyly.

Toni Morrison was the first African-American woman to receive the Nobel Prize in literature. Her father worked at the steel mill while her mother raised the kids. Morrison said about her mother:

"When an eviction notice was put on our house, she tore it off. If there were maggots in our flour, she wrote a letter to Franklin Roosevelt. My mother believed something should be done about inhuman situations."

Morrison went to college, got interested in theater and traveled around in an acting troupe, then went on to get a master's in English. She loved to read, but had never been a writer except for a few stories in high school. But after she got married and had two children, her marriage started to dissolve, and she needed an escape.

She said:

"It was as though I had nothing left but my imagination. I wrote like someone with a dirty habit. Secretly. Compulsively. Shyly."

After joining a writing group, she wrote a story about a black girl who wanted blue eyes. And then she started to expand it into a novel called, *The Bluest Eye* (1969). She went on to write eight more novels, including *Song of Solomon* (1977), *Beloved* (1987), and *A Mercy* (2008).

Do you write secretly, compulsively, slyly? If not, I highly recommend it. Sometimes secrets are good, especially if there are critics nearby or you can be easily influenced. Part of the task of being a writer is to protect your new creations. Some of you may do things totally differently, but I know that if I start sharing something I've written too soon, the piece loses energy. So I don't talk about or share anything I'm writing until I have completed an entire first draft.

Are You Resilient?

According to the American Heritage College Dictionary I keep near my desk, the definition of resilience is: *the ability to spring back and recover quickly after being bent, stretched or compressed.*

Let's face it, life has a way of bending, stretching and compressing us, even when we do our best to avoid it. Resiliency is a trait that can be helpful to everyone on the planet. But it can be especially helpful to writers, artists, and creative types.

Artists (and people with artistic sensibilities) are often bent, stretched or compressed by rejection, society's lack of interest, and/or the critics within and without. But I think the roots of resiliency go deeper than just being able to bounce back after criticism and rejection. I think it can also involve a basic attitude about life. In my mind, resilient people have several characteristics in common.

They basically have:

1. a positive outlook on life
2. a sense of a bigger purpose at play in their lives
3. a certain level of trust in themselves and the processes of life
4. flexibility when life throws a curve ball
5. an ability to keep going in the face of fear

6. an ability to find many solutions to a problem
7. an acceptance of diversity and differences
8. a desire to grow and change

On a scale of 1 – 10 where do you fall?

1 = "I'm not the least bit resilient."
10 = "I'm the most resilient person I've ever known."

I feel like I'm at about a 7.5. But I'm working to get that number even higher. Where do you fall on the scale? What's one small thing you can do to increase your resilience?

Resolutions for Writers That Might Truly, Deeply Change Your Life

Often our New Year's resolutions lack the liveliness that we need for them to take root in us and many times we're unsuccessful with them.

What if instead of taking away something from your life (like added pounds or cigarettes) your New Year's resolutions were strictly about adding vitality to your life? With that in mind, I came up with some resolutions that might help you in your writing endeavors.

Pick one, pick a dozen or simply enjoy the list below of possible resolutions that could make a difference in your writing life. Then take it a step farther and get specific. For example, based on the first suggestion, what might choosing kindness over criticism look like? Maybe once a day you stop yourself from making a critical comment and say something positive to someone instead.

- Choose kindness over criticism.
- Experience beauty daily.
- Expand your talent. If you write novels try writing a short story or try writing a poem.
- Share your talents with the world. Go to an open mic, submit to small publications.

- Grow genuine self-confidence and forgive yourself for imperfections.
- Give genuine compliments, either in person or in writing.
- Act courageous, even when you're frightened.
- Be receptive to new ways of doing things.
- Go outside and appreciate trees at least once a week.
- Cultivate simple pleasures.
- Be playful.
- Love more people, more often.
- Communicate to key people what a difference they've made in your life.
- Give only heartfelt gifts or something you make yourself.
- Commit to relationships that have a wide capacity for love and acceptance.
- Rest well. Get at least 7 hours of sleep a night and take naps on weekends.
- Cultivate your sense of humor. Laugh at least 3 times a day.
- Allow yourself to be inspired.
- Embrace new positive patterns. Smile more. Frown less.
- Exercise compassion with someone who drives you nuts.

- Tell a story that captivates your audience.
- Seek out wise people and listen to what they have to say.
- Read really good poetry out loud.
- Listen to really good music.
- Write a poem a day, even if it's a bad draft.
- Write the first draft of a novel without tinkering.
- Write a country song.
- Play a musical instrument badly.
- Paint a birdhouse, a landscape, a family portrait—the more primitive the better.
- Photograph something beautiful outdoors.
- Dance to the radio.
- Do something creative every day. Anything.
- Breathe deeply. Inhale Life. Exhale Gratitude.

Perseverance

One thing that it is commonly agreed upon at writers and artists conferences and in books about craft is that those who somehow make it in the art and book world are those who possess one trait above all others: perseverance.

A recent *New York Times* article by Deborah Sontag entitled "At 94, She's the Hot New Thing in Painting," solidifies this point.

In an era when the art and writing worlds idolize, and often richly reward, the young and the new, Carmen Herrara, age 94, *"embodies a different, much rarer kind of success, that of the artist long overlooked by the market, and by history, who persevered because she had no choice."*

In the article it tells of a time when her good friend, the painter Tony Bechara, raised a glass.

"We have a saying in Puerto Rico," he said. *"The bus — la guagua — always comes for those who wait."*

The Cuban-born Ms. Herrera, laughed gustily, and responded, *"Well, Tony, I've been at the bus stop for 94 years!"*

In Carmen Herrera's own words:

"I do it because I have to do it; it's a compulsion that also gives me pleasure. I never in my life had any idea of money and I thought fame was a very vulgar thing. So I just worked and waited. And at the end of my life, I'm getting a lot of recognition, to my amazement and my pleasure, actually."

How many of us have this level of stamina and perseverance, this level of dedication to our art? Hopefully, you won't have to wait 94 years, but how long are you willing to wait at that bus stop for your creative talents to be recognized?

Take Wrong Turns

Author Alice Munro, known for her short stories, grew up on a farm in Ontario.

She said:

"Reading was an indulgence that you didn't go in for if there was physical work to be done."

Women were only supposed to read on Sundays, because on every other day of the week they had no excuse to be reading when they could be knitting instead. So as a kid, she was always telling herself stories, and when she didn't like the endings — like in Hans Christian Andersen's "The Little Mermaid" — she would make up new ones.

She went to college, hoping to become a writer, but she dropped out to get married and have three children. She got divorced and went back to her hometown to take care of her sick father, and she was amazed at how much material there was in her little town.

She also said:

"What I wanted was every last thing, every layer of speech and thought, stroke of light on bark or walls, every smell, pothole, pain, crack, delusion, held still and held together — radiant, everlasting."

And so she took those things, and turned them into short stories. She has written 11 books of short stories, and a new collection, *Too Much Happiness*.

Here's her advice to aspiring writers:

"It's not possible to advise a young writer because every young writer is so different. You might say, 'Read,' but a writer can read too much and be paralyzed. Or, 'Don't read, don't think, just write,' and the result could be a mountain of drivel. If you're going to be a writer you'll probably take a lot of wrong turns and then one day just end up writing something you have to write, then getting it better and better just because you want it to be better, and even when you get old and think 'There must be something else people do,' you won't quite be able to quit."

More Great Quotes about Writing and Creativity

"Success is a finished book, a stack of pages each of which is filled with words. If you reach that point, you have won a victory over yourself no less impressive than sailing single-handed around the world."
— Tom Clancy

"Most of the basic material a writer works with is acquired before the age of fifteen." — Willa Cather

"Confront the dark parts of yourself. … Your willingness to wrestle with your demons will cause your angels to sing." — August Wilson

"It's none of their business that you have to learn to write. Let them think you were born that way."
— Ernest Hemingway

"I try to create sympathy for my characters, then turn the monsters loose." — Stephen King

"You can't wait for inspiration. You have to go after it with a club."
— Jack London

"When your heart speaks, take good notes."
– Judith Campbell

"Adopt the pace of nature; her secret is patience."
– Ralph Waldo Emerson

"The Power of imagination makes us infinite."
– John Muir

"We have an obligation to use the language. To push ourselves: to find out what words mean and how to deploy them, to communicate clearly, to say what we mean."
– Neil Gaiman

Attitude of Gratitude

When those rejections are pouring in or a bad review knocks the breath right out of you, creating a gratitude list can help return you to a sense of power and possibility. Here are 100 things (in no particular order) that I am grateful for:

1. my mate
2. my children
3. friends
4. meaningful work
5. laughter
6. community
7. mountain bluebirds
8. coffee shops
9. organic Assam tea
10. road maps
11. wildlife protection
12. trails
13. libraries
14. bookstores
15. artists
16. painters
17. wisdom

18. knowledge
19. potluck dinners
20. National Parks
21. prairie dogs and coyotes
22. good movies
23. elk
24. waterfalls
25. imagination
26. boldness
27. courage
28. people who read books
29. people who read my books
30. discipline
31. joy
32. poetry
33. encouragement
34. mountain ranges
35. good physical health
36. poets
37. dancers
38. integrity
39. sparrows
40. eagles
41. porch swings
42. honor
43. faith
44. resilience

45. kindness
46. authenticity
47. aspiring writers, artists, poets
48. cottonwood trees
49. sparrows
50. shade
51. oak trees
52. all trees
53. extended family
54. unconditional love
55. inspiration
56. strawberries
57. gardens
58. water hoses
59. Pentel mechanical pencils
60. streams
61. rivers
62. oceans
63. mother earth
64. adversity
65. inner work
66. good neighbors
67. surprising moments
68. Pentel pens
69. fresh baked bread
70. blueberries
71. raspberries

72. vegetables
73. art galleries
74. resiliency
75. rain forests
76. vacations
77. a really good joke
78. creativity
79. traveling
80. pets
81. teachers
82. mentors
83. really good books
84. children
85. literary agents
86. bird feeders
87. dreams
88. snow
89. snowshoes
90. snow shovels
91. running water
92. electricity
93. shelter
94. honest politicians
95. really good music
96. spiritual paths
97. sidewalks
98. word processing software

99. time to write
100. hope

Fieldwork: Write your own gratitude list. It doesn't have to be the ultimate list for your whole life, just what you are grateful for right now.

Fake It Till You Make It

Sometimes as writers, artists and other creative types, the ultimate challenge is in believing in ourselves and believing that we have something to say, especially when we're starting out.

When I look back over my writing life so far, I can see that my belief and my confidence in myself as a writer came slowly as a result of consistently writing and learning my craft. Over the years I've taken writing classes and read numerous books on how to improve my writing and gone to writing conferences that focus more on craft than marketing. Mostly, however, I've spent time practicing my craft and writing. Confidence has come from years of writing and years of improving.

Writers who believe in themselves have self-respect and a sense of purpose. They have a desire to put something good and lasting out into the world. They tend to look at their efforts with a non-judgmental, compassionate eye. They tell their inner critic to take a hike!

Writers who believe in themselves forgive themselves for being imperfect. You'd be amazed how much we grasp at perfection, but it's just impossible.

You know the saying: *Fake it till you make it*. If you aren't as confident and believing in yourself as you'd like, this may be something you want to try. Imagine how a writer who believes in herself would act. Imagine how a writer with great confidence would act. Sometimes acting *as if* is the most powerful exercise we can do.

The Gift that Revives the Soul

I am a champion of creativity and creative types, offering encouragement to all manner of artists, whether they are writers, painters, poets, dancers, sculptors, or people whose creativity (or inner artist) has not yet found an outlet.

Below is an excerpt from a book I read by Lewis Hyde entitled *The Gift: Creativity and the Artist in the Modern World*. See if it makes sense to you.

"The art that matters to us—which moves the heart, or revives the soul, or delights the senses, or offers courage for living, however we choose to describe the experience—that work is received by us as a gift is received. Even if we have paid a fee at the door of the museum or concert hall, when we are touched by a work of art something comes to us which has nothing to do with the price. I went to see a landscape painter's works, and that evening, walking among pine trees near my home, I could see the shapes and colors I had not seen the day before. The spirit of an artist's gifts can wake our own....Our sense of harmony can hear the harmonies that Mozart heard. We may not have the power to profess our gifts as the artist does, and yet we come to recognize, and in a sense to receive the endowments of our being through the agency of his/her creation. We feel fortunate, even redeemed...the gift revives the soul. When we are moved by art

we are grateful that the artist lived, thankful that she labored in the service of her gifts."

Are you laboring in the service of your gifts? Have you experienced art lately that revived your soul, delighted your senses, or offered you courage for living? If not, I hope you'll go in search of it.

Our Deepest Fear

As Marianne Williamson is often quoted as saying:

"Our deepest fear is not that we are inadequate. Our deepest fear is that we are powerful beyond measure. It is our light, not our darkness that most frightens us. We ask ourselves, Who am I to be brilliant, gorgeous, talented, fabulous? Actually, who are you not *to be? You are a child of God. Your playing small does not serve the world. There is nothing enlightened about shrinking so that other people won't feel insecure around you. We are all meant to shine, as children do. We were born to make manifest the glory of God that is within us. It's not just in some of us; it's in everyone. And as we let our own light shine, we unconsciously give other people permission to do the same. As we are liberated from our own fear, our presence automatically liberates others."*

"Playing" small doesn't help anyone. You are meant to shine!

Keeping the Channel Open

Here's a powerful quote from Martha Graham to her student Agnes de Mille, found in de Mille's memoir, *Dance to the Piper*.

"There is a vitality, a life force, a quickening that is translated through you into action, and because there is only one of you in all time, the expression is unique. And if you block it, it will never exist through any other medium . . . and be lost. The world will not have it.

"It is not your business to determine how good it is nor how valuable it is; nor how it compares with other expressions. It is your business to keep it yours clearly and directly, to keep the channel open.

"You do not even have to believe in yourself or your work. You have to keep open and aware directly to the urges that motivate YOU. Keep the channel open....No artist is pleased....There is no satisfaction whatever at any time. There is only a queer, divine dissatisfaction: a blessed unrest that keeps us marching and makes us more alive."

May we all keep the channel open for the work that is uniquely ours to complete.

It's Never Too Late to Start Your Writing Career

Ilene Beckerman, an advertising exec-turned-writer, didn't begin her writing career until the age of 60, when she wrote and illustrated a book for her five children to remember her by.

She said: *"My purpose was to say things to my children one doesn't have the time to say. I wanted them to know I wasn't always their mother. I was a girl, I had best friends, we did stupid things together. I was on a bus with my friend once eating dog bones so people would look at us. I wanted them to know."*

As the story goes, she took the book she'd written to her ad agency to use the photocopy machines. After making a dozen copies for her children and a few close friends, she put them in big red binders, with the illustrations she'd sketched in plastic sheet protectors. Unknown to her, the friend of a friend sent one of the binders over to Algonquin Books and her self-made book was picked up for publication.

Love, Loss, and What I Wore was published in 1995. It is a memoir and tells the story of her life growing up in Manhattan in the 1930s, '40s, and '50s. Drawings of the clothes that she was wearing during that time were included. The book also contains advice from her grandmother, who raised her. Here's one:

"If you have to stand on your head to make somebody happy, all you can expect is a big headache."

And:

"It's better to be alone than with someone who makes you feel lonely." And, *"You never know what goes on behind closed doors, even Miss America can have hemorrhoids."*

And:

"If beauty brought happiness, Elizabeth Taylor wouldn't have needed so many husbands."

Since then, she has written and illustrated *What We Do for Love* (1997), *Makeovers at the Beauty Counter of Happiness* (2005) — containing unsent letters to Marilyn Monroe, Mother Teresa, Audrey Hepburn, Sarah Jessica Parker, and her own 11-year-old granddaughter — and *Mother of the Bride* (2000), about planning her daughter's wedding. She said:

"Childbirth was a lot easier than being the mother of the bride."

The book that originally began as twelve photocopies has now sold over 100,000 copies all over the world.

Things To Do While The Economy Sucks

The economy sucks. Maybe you've lost your job or you're simply looking for something to do since you can't afford to go anywhere right now. I have a suggestion. **Maybe it's time to write that book that you've talked about writing for the last ten or twenty years.**

Nearly every time I give a book signing or a reading someone inevitably walks up to me to announce that they want to write a book someday. Sometimes they'll say they have the idea for the book, they just haven't had the time to put it on paper. Sometimes they'll even tell me their idea to see if I want to write it.

(Please know that I will never take you up on this suggestion. I follow my own muse and like to develop my own ideas.)

But now, as the economy and our lives go through major restructuring, it may be the perfect time to get started. It requires absolutely no money up front. Most of us have a computer and know how to open a Word document. If we don't, nearly all of our wonderful community libraries have computers and kind people there to show you how to work them. Or at the very least, most of us have paper and pens lying around the house, if not cocktail napkins and the backs of the envelopes of those bills you haven't been able to pay.

Once you get started, you can tell your family and friends, as well as your online following, that you can't go to the unemployment office right now because you're working on your book. If anything, saying this may give you a much needed boost of self-esteem. After all, you aren't sitting around watching Project Runway, CNN or The View; you're tapping into your artistic talent. This is an investment in yourself that can pay great dividends down the road.

I'm not really suggesting that you shirk off your responsibilities. I'm just wondering if, for some of us, this time might offer an opportunity within the crisis.

Of course, nothing is easy. The journey from first word on the page to a finished manuscript that is good enough to be submitted to literary agents, editors and publishers is a multiple stepped process. Even if you decide to self-publish, you need a good, well-written product or your mother will be the only one buying it.

Whether you write literary fiction, mysteries, thrillers, science fiction, women's fiction, memoir or non-fiction, the process of writing that book can take months, even years, to complete. And even then, there are no guarantees. But you might as well get started while you have a little time and see where the path takes you. You may surprise yourself.

Writing is as much an act of self-discovery as anything else. It's never a wasted activity, whatever the final outcome.

Top 5 Tips for Aspiring Writers, Plus One

Many people dream of writing the great American novel. It's a beautiful dream and here are my top five tips for making it a reality.

1. As with any profession or craft, becoming excellent is simple but not easy. The best advice I can give to writers starting out is to READ. Read very well-written books in the genre you want to write in. I heard this advice at the very first writer's conference I ever attended many years ago, as well as the most recent one I attended, and it has served me well.

One presenter, who has written dozens of books and is at the top of his field, even suggested that writers starting out **read 100 books** of whatever kind you want to write, before you even start writing. I heard gasps in the room when he said this. I have a somewhat softer take on that. I think you can start counting down the hundred while you are starting to write.

2. Take classes. It's helpful to take classes or go to conferences or join a writer's group (or several until you find the right one). You don't necessarily need an MFA, but do take advantage of the numerous local, regional and national conferences and workshops held throughout the year for writers.

3. Join a writer's group. A writer's group was incredibly helpful to me when I wrote my first novel, *Seeking Sara Summers*. I had written novels for children before, but when it came to writing my first novel for adults it seemed a daunting task. To help me accomplish my goal, I joined a small writer's group of only six people, including myself. At the very first meeting I told them that I wanted to bring a chapter of a new novel to them (a really rough draft) every time we met, which was every two weeks. This broke the task into smaller, more achievable goals. I kept my promise and had an entire first draft finished within a year.

4. Hire a freelance editor to clean up your manuscript when you're finished. An editor can do anything from line editing for typos and grammatical corrections all the way up to substantial editing around style, characterization, plot, etc. When you're starting out, it's a good investment to get more substantial editing to help you improve.

5. Read books on writing. There isn't just one book about how to write that I would recommend. There are so many out there. I have a shelf full of them myself. Some can be quite helpful, like *Immediate Fiction* by Jerry Cleaver and *Writing the Breakthrough Novel* by Donald Maas (these of course are more for fiction writers). *Wired for Story* by Lisa Cron is really interesting about how our brains need stories. Two books I like for

memoir writers are *Your Life as Story* by Tristine Rainer and *Handling the Truth* by Beth Kephart.

I can honestly say that what has made me a better writer is to practice the craft **every day**. Get words on the page, even if it's just a few, and don't let anybody or anything, including your own negative thoughts, stop you.

Whatever kind of book you're writing, keep at it. We humans love and need good stories, so **just do it!**

More Favorite Quotes about Writing and Creativity

"It is harrowing for me to try to teach 20-year-old students, who earnestly want to improve their writing. The best I can think to tell them is: Quit smoking, and observe posted speed limits. This will improve your odds of getting old enough to be wise."
– Barbara Kingsolver

"Writing is the only thing that, when I do it, I don't feel I should be doing something else." – Gloria Steinem

"There is only one thing written for its own sake, and that is a shopping list; everything else we write in order to say something to somebody."
– Umberto Eco

It is to the silence you should listen
the silence behind invocations, allusions
the silence of rhetoric . . .
What I have written
I have written between the lines.
– Gunnar Ekelof

"Every person is born into life as a blank page- and every person leaves life as a full book. Our lives are our story, and our story is our life." – Christina Baldwin

"I live with the people I create and it has always made my essential loneliness less keen." – Carson McCullers

"Imagination is more important than knowledge."
– Albert Einstein

"Go confidently in the direction of your dreams. Live the life you have imagined." – Henry David Thoreau

Muse It or Lose It

How often do you get one of those truly great ideas in life and you forget to write it down? So many good ideas, even epiphanies, come to us at inconvenient times: the middle of the night, the middle of a meeting, in the shower, or whenever. Our muse has a mind and a schedule of her own that doesn't always respect or honor our timing of things.

As Sam Horn, author of *Pop! Stand Out in Any Crowd,* says about our muse: *"All it asks is that when it gives us an idea, we write it down. As long as we do, it'll keep coming around."*

For this article, I have borrowed her phrase: *Muse It Or Lose It*. Horn also has a section in her book called: Ink It When You Think It.

As I've mentioned before, I had not planned on writing *The Secret Sense of Wildflower*. In fact, I swore to myself, as someone born and raised in the southern United States, that I would never, *ever,* write southern fiction. I had enough scary, weird characters in my gene pool. I didn't feel the need to explore all the dynamics in a novel. But *never say never*, as the cliché goes.

In the middle of the night, several years ago now, a voice began speaking in my imagination. It was the main character of this novel I swore I would never write, telling me her story.

In fact, she was practically dictating the book to me. I have had enough experience with characters and ideas showing up that I knew that if I didn't get up and start writing it down that I would lose it. In fact, this character might even find some other writer to tell her story to. So even though I could have really used that night's sleep and the year or so that followed where I was carefully working and reworking her story, I feel good that I took responsibility for it.

I know all this sounds a little crazy, but I'm southern; I feel like I'm allowed. I'm also an ex-shrink so I know I'm not dealing with mental illness, just the process of creativity, which sometimes mirrors mental issues. There is something very mysterious about how stories and ideas are born. After over a decade of writing, I'm almost convinced that they choose us, instead of us choosing them.

Mystery aside, and on the purely practical end of things, it's important to write things down. Anne Lamott, devotes a whole chapter in her book *Bird by Bird: Some Instructions on Writing and Life,* to the use of 3x5 index cards. She is never without them. Of course this doesn't work for everybody. You may prefer a note pad or want to use your Smartphone or have the memory of an elephant and never need to write anything down. But it is crucial to take action and claim it.

When you get an idea for an article or a story, or you start hearing a stream of dialogue in your imagination, you are being given a gift. Think twice before you turn down this gift because it may not return. I truly believe that if you honor your muse, your muse will honor you.

What Are You Missing?

There's a great story that first appeared in the Washington Post, in an article written by Gene Weingarten, called "Pearls Before Breakfast."

A man stood inside a metro station in Washington DC and started to play the violin; it was a cold January morning. He played six Bach pieces for about 45 minutes. During that time, since it was rush hour, it was calculated that a thousand people went through the station, most of them on their way to work.

Three minutes went by and a middle aged man noticed there was musician playing. He slowed his pace and stopped for a few seconds and then hurried up to meet his schedule.

A minute later, the violinist received his first dollar tip: a woman threw the money in the till and without stopping continued to walk.

A few minutes later, someone leaned against the wall to listen to him, but the man looked at his watch and started to walk again. Clearly he was late for work.

The one who paid the most attention was a 3 year old boy. His mother tagged him along, hurried but the kid stopped to look at the violinist. Finally the mother pushed hard and the child continued to walk turning his head all the time. This action was repeated by several other children. All the parents, without exception, forced them to move on.

In the 45 minutes the musician played, only 6 people stopped and stayed for a while. About 20 gave him money but continued to walk their normal pace. He collected $32. When he finished playing and silence took over, no one noticed it. No one applauded, nor was there any recognition.

No one knew this but the violinist was Joshua Bell, one of the best musicians in the world. He played one of the most intricate pieces ever written, with a violin worth 3.5 million dollars.

Two days before his playing in the subway, Joshua Bell sold out at a theater in Boston at $100 a ticket.

This is a real story. Joshua Bell playing incognito in the metro station was organized by the Washington Post as part of a social experiment about perception, taste and priorities of people. The outlines were: in a commonplace environment at an inappropriate hour.

When do we perceive beauty? Do we stop to appreciate it? Do we recognize the talent in an unexpected context?

One of the possible conclusions from this experience could be: **If we do not have a moment to stop and listen to one of the best musicians in the world playing the best music ever written, how many other things are we missing?**

P.S. I have been fortunate enough to see Joshua Bell play in concert. He is truly a wonderful musician. Even if he was disguised as a street musician, I would like to think I would have stopped to listen. But maybe if I was on my way to work, and was running late, who knows. How much do we miss if we don't allow ourselves to be pulled in by the wonder of the moment?

Do You Have "Barnum In Your Bones"?

For those of you who are aching to hear something about marketing and creating a platform, I offer you this story. Keep in mind, however, that your first and only task is to write! Too many writers today are building platforms to nowhere. You have to have written something for this to make sense. Got it?

Back in 1996, Brad Meltzer built what was arguably the first author web site for his first novel, *Tenth Justice*, including character interviews and the first chapter. His publisher thought he was nuts.

> *"The publishing world is very resistant to change," Meltzer said. "But there are always people — mostly the young and the hungry — who are trying new things. The days of just holing up and writing in solitude are gone. Today, you can't be a successful writer without having a little Barnum in your bones."*

> *"But, I want to write in solitude,"* we writers say. *"Don't tell me those days are gone!"*

I love solitude. I love those hours of total absorption with the creative process. But I actually think Meltzer is right. Once we have written the best book we possibly can, all the while developing our craft, and said book is ready to be traditionally or self-published, then we have to have, at least a tiny bit, of P.T. Barnum in our bones if we expect even a modicum of success in today's publishing world. Barnum was one of the world's greatest promoters.

This isn't an easy task for many of us. As I've said before, writers are typically introverts. That's how we can spend so much time alone developing our characters (our poems, our articles) and creating our stories. But we also have to figure out ways to get our talents out into the world, albeit in small arenas or large.

We must call upon an extroverted function to put ourselves out there—to secure our literary agents, to publish our books, to develop our websites, then to participate in interviews, book clubs, etc.

So what do you think? Do you have enough of the "Big Top" in you to go for that writing career? Do you even think it's necessary to have this skill-set to be a success? Whatever your answer, I wish you every success.

Follow your Bliss

Henry Sapoznik is a musician who has a pure and shining love of, as he says, *"music that sounds like it comes from somewhere."* He was recently interviewed by the Burry Man Writers Center had this to say about his work:

"I don't do my work for anyone but me. This is a completely selfish undertaking. I love people to like what I do, but I can't worry, will people like this? I love my audience, but they gotta love what I do. If we forget, if we're not moved by our own work, our compasses are all screwed up. My work is completely reflective of my own interests—'oh, this amuses me, I wonder what this would be like?' . . . and we're off to the races. I can't even imagine a world where we're forced to forgo that creative process. Maybe we're stuck in a juvenile frame of mind that the world is about us."

Sapoznik also said that doing the work was about satisfying his own integrity. It's as if he trusts the process completely, even if, for the moment, it doesn't seem to be taking him anywhere.

When you create, whether it's writing, painting or some other art form, are you doing it for yourself? Do you love what you are doing and creating? I agree with Sapoznik that these are great "acid test" questions, ones we want to ask ourselves with regularity.

And what if you get lost in your work? So lost, maybe, that you aren't sure just what you are doing or why?

Sapoznik said:

"It's like the thing I learned in the Boy Scouts: if you get lost, stay where you are. You will be found."

In my mind, this translates to all of us former Girl Scouts, too. *Follow your bliss*, Joseph Campbell used to say. And if in pursuit of your bliss you lose your way, don't panic. The bliss will find *you*.

The Place of the Artist

"I see little of more importance to the future of our country than full recognition of the place of the artist. If art is to nourish our culture, society must set the artist free to follow his vision wherever it takes him."

— John F. Kennedy

10,000 Hours

10,000 hours of concentrated effort is what it takes to become an expert at or a master of something, says Malcolm Gladwell in his book, *Outliers*. If this is true, it is interesting information. I wonder how many hours all the would-be writers and artists and poets I know actually put into their craft. For some reason, many writers expect success to happen overnight. My first ten years writing, I expected this, too. But what if success is not so much about talent as it is about practice?

As I mentioned earlier, I kept a log book for years documenting the amount of time I spent writing. I did this for two reasons: 1) so that I would see writing as a real job and 2) to hold myself accountable. According to Malcolm and the hours I have amassed, I have crossed over into expert status.

When I look back at what I was writing 10 years ago, I can see how far I've come. I also know that with another 10,000 hours under my belt, I'll be a lot better than I am now. Yet, I do find it fascinating that I find myself coming into my own as a writer now, with that amount of time put into my craft. Could there really be something to this 10,000 hours concept? If nothing else, a bar to reach for?

So if you're a beginning writer, it may be a little soon to win the National Book Award, but keep going. Your time spent writing is not wasted time. Put in the writing hours you need to develop your mastery!

7 Awesome Quotes about Creativity

Here are my **top 7 favorite quotes** about creativity.

"Life is a great big canvas; throw all the paint you can at it."
– Danny Kaye

"And so our mothers and grandmothers have, more often than not anonymously, handed on the creative spark, the seed of the flower they themselves never hoped to see -- or like a sealed letter they could not plainly read."
– Alice Walker

"The secret to being a writer is that you have to write. It's not enough to think about writing or to study literature or plan a future life as an author. You really have to lock yourself away, alone, and get to work."
– Augusten Burroughs

"We don't need lists of rights and wrongs, tables of do's and don'ts: we need books, time, and silence. 'Thou shalt not' is soon forgotten, but 'Once upon a time' lasts forever." – Philip Pullman

"All art is autobiographical; the pearl is the oyster's autobiography."
– Federico Fellini

"Make visible what, without you, might never have been seen."
– Robert Bresson

"Talent is not talent until it is shared." – fortune cookie

A League of Our Own

Sometimes life is just hard. For me, writing a book and putting it out into the world is one of the hardest things I've ever done. Mainly because I've spent a great deal of my life trying not to draw attention to myself. Why? Because being out in the open, at least while growing up, meant danger. Safety was found in introversion and quietness.

Childhood history is not always easy to overcome. Yet despite the obstacles, I have been determined to keep challenging myself to put my work out into the world. I think of it as stepping into my greatness.

In the movie, *A League of Their Own*, the star of a women's professional baseball team, played by Geena Davis, wants to leave the team before its season ends to return home with her husband.

When the team's coach, played by Tom Hanks, challenges her decision and wonders why, she says, *"It just got too hard."*

Hanks replies, *"It's supposed to be hard. If it wasn't hard, everyone would do it—the hard is what makes it great."*

We've all had things that we've wanted to give up on. And, like me, you've probably given up on a few.

But what is it that you need to **not** give up on?

What is it that you need to do that is hard, and its hardness makes it great?

Are you ready to step into your greatness?

Dare To Compete

A few years ago I read Hillary Clinton's book, *Living History*. There was a section near the end where she talked about the agonizing decision about whether or not she should make a campaign run to be a senator for New York. Her friends were advising against it, the press was going wild with speculation and exploring every negative aspect of the possibility. Yet still she debated whether this would be the right move for her. Her decision still unmade, she attended an event in New York City that was to honor an HBO film called "Dare to Compete" about the challenges for women in sports.

Sofia Totti, the captain of the girls' basketball team featured in the HBO film, had the honor of introducing Hillary Clinton to the crowd. When Hillary walked to the podium she and the young woman shook hands and Sofia leaned toward her and whispered in her ear:

"Dare to compete, Mrs. Clinton, dare to compete."

Hillary Clinton wrote about this as a defining moment. In her own words:

"Her comment caught me off guard, so much so that I left the event and began to think: Could I be afraid to do something I had urged countless other women to do? Why am I vacillating about taking on this race? Why aren't I thinking more seriously about it? Maybe I should 'dare to compete.'"

We all know where this attitude took Hillary Clinton in the years that followed. She not only became a formidable senator but dared to compete for the presidential nomination of the Democratic Party and then dared to be Secretary of State. As she has said, as well as many others, Hillary Clinton's bold move put millions of cracks in a glass ceiling that limits the daring of women.

Is there something that you can apply this challenge to? Is there something you need to *dare to compete* about? If so, maybe it's time to try it. Who knows where it might lead!

A Lesson from Harriet Tubman

Harriet Tubman, a former slave, escaped to freedom on the Underground Railroad. She returned many times to lead other slaves to that same freedom. She endured tremendous hardship, fears and doubts. But she had a flame blazing inside her that kept her going and she helped hundreds find that same fire to keep going in the face of daunting opposition. She wrote:

"If you're tired, keep going. If you are scared, keep going. If you are hungry, keep going. If you want a taste of freedom, keep going."

You and I are blessed not to be literally enslaved. Yet, most of us are enslaved in psychological ways. So what is it that you need to be free of? Is it a poverty mentality? (This is hard not to have in our current economy, by the way.)

Or is it an oppressive attitude that limits you? In the psychotherapy world where I used to practice, we called this the *inner critic*.

Is it a physically limitation you are working hard to overcome? Or have you been pursuing your dreams but with little success?

Whatever it is that is keeping you enslaved, can be overcome. Call on your own inner Harriet Tubman. Call on that brave part of you that will do whatever you need to do to get free. Join the *psychic* Underground Railroad. We can all get free together.

Keep going!

A Different Kind of Empty Nest

I want my children to leave home. My book children, at least. I have been working on getting some of them out of my house for years. They are the manuscripts that I have nurtured and revised from upstarts into full-fledged stories.

It's not easy getting your "children" to leave home. I know a writer who has written an entire novel and has kept it under her bed for years. I have no doubt that it is an excellent novel because she is a thoughtful, excellent writer. But something stops her from taking the risk of putting it out into the world.

My theory, and I could be wrong, is that she is afraid to get her work out there because she then runs the risk of it being criticized. At least while it is under her bed she is safe.

I understand this fear, however, I don't believe it is useful. As artists, and parents, we must put our creations out into the world or we run the risk of crippling them. It is our responsibility, after we have done our job to the best of our ability, to release these creations so that they have an opportunity to live out their destiny. We must release them because we never know who we might help or who might be encouraged and inspired by our words.

So I say to my own book children still at home: It is time to take flight. If you fail, you fail. If you succeed, you succeed. Either way, I have fulfilled my part of the promise.

Is there anything that you haven't sent out into the world that you really need to? A book? An article? A painting? A poem you want to submit? If so, I encourage you to let your talents take flight. Give them the chance to spread their wings and fly, bearing their gifts to those who need them.

Top 5 Favorite Quotes of All Time

I hope you love these quotes as much as I do. It's obvious I have a lot of favorites. So here are my top 5 picks for **all time**. At least for now!

"Do one thing every day that scares you."
— Eleanor Roosevelt

"It is difficult to get the news from poems, yet men die miserably every day for lack of what is found there."
— William Carlos Williams

"The seed cannot sprout upwards without simultaneously sending roots into the ground."
— Proverb from an ancient Egyptian temple

"For poems are not words, after all, but fires for the cold, ropes let down to the lost, something as necessary as bread in the pockets of the hungry." — Mary Oliver

"Not only the thirsty seek the water, the water as well seeks the thirsty." — Rumi

Never Say Never

I grew up in the southeastern United States where it seems there is a Baptist Church on every corner and confederate flags hanging in the back windows of passing pickup trucks. Although I've read my fair share of William Faulkner, Eudora Welty and Reynolds Price, as well as others, Southern fiction and Southern writers were just not something that excited me. Perhaps it was because I grew up with "characters" around me that I wanted to forget.

Needless to say, with this attitude, when I became a writer I swore that I would **never, ever** write a "Southern" novel. I wanted to divorce myself from the South and from its sometimes backward ways. I wanted to write literary fiction, which in mind did not include anything Southern. And yet, like many of us, what I set out to avoid, is exactly what I found myself doing with my novel, *The Secret Sense of Wildflower*. It is considered "southern gothic" literature, although any true Southerner would call it normal, everyday life.

So the old cliché of "never say never" stands. Life, as I've said before, seems to have its own ideas about what might be best for us and has a much bigger imagination than we do.

What have you avoided that might hold unexpected riches?

Defying the Odds

At the first writer's conference I ever attended one brave presenter, a woman who had authored a dozen books, said: *Writing is the get-rich-slow plan.* Of course this is not what I wanted to hear. As a single-mom and first time writer I wanted, in fact needed, a *get-rich-quick plan.*

Over a decade later, I can vouch that what she said is true. At least for now. However there are always those writers who defy the odds. Sometimes they are simply lucky and were in the *right place at the right time,* as the saying goes. At other times they were able to write a story and create characters that captured the imagination of an entire culture with books like *Harry Potter, Twilight* and *The Hunger Games.*

I invite you to defy the odds and write a really great story, memoir or work of nonfiction. Write something that is memorable and captures a reader's imagination.

Defy the odds!

Coming Out of the Closet as a Writer

Over the years I have slowly "come out" of the closet as a writer. I have gotten braver with each passing year, as if I am slowly earning the right to be myself. However, whenever someone asks me what I do and I tell them, I often get from them a sort-of glazed-over look, as if I am the third person to identify themselves that way today.

Their eyes narrow slightly and I imagine them wondering: *Is she a serious writer? Or is this just a passing phase? Aunt Mildred had a passing phase. She wrote silly poems about woodchucks....*

Then, as the glaze begins to clear, I see a secondary thought: *But she looks so normal.*

To say that I have books finally out creates new responses by those unfamiliar with my journey. A sort of smile masked with skepticism. *Doesn't everyone have a book out these days?* this smile says. Or at least everyone they know is writing a book, or wanting to write a book, or maybe even considering reading one.

Do we label ourselves to makes things easier for us or for other people? If I say I am a writer, then I allow whoever is listening to entertain their preconceived notion of what that means. Like if someone tells me they are an accountant or a lawyer, I have a sense of what their life is like. Or I like to think I have a sense of what their life is like. Actually, I have no idea.

I wonder sometimes if labels are helpful at all. Perhaps it makes sense to use them on complicated processed foods, or medicines. But other things in nature don't label themselves. The woodchucks Aunt Mildred wrote about do not pontificate, *I think, therefore, I am . . . a woodchuck. A woodchuck who chucks wood.* I venture to say that woodchucks are simply what they are, and they give no thought to whether they are a slender woodchuck, or a woodchuck that could lose a few pounds, and really should join the water ballet class at the pond.

What must this be like, to simply be who we are without pretense or fear? Perhaps, when this glazed-over life finally clears, we will know. And then we will each have our own coming out story. A coming out to our authentic selves as writers.

Life Has a Much Bigger Imagination Than We Do

I was with a wonderful group of people one weekend who came together for a house-warming. A circle of friends, new and old, gathered around a large dining room table to talk and warm this space. On the table sat a landscape blueprint for the large backyard that the former owners of the home had left undeveloped.

Throughout the afternoon all of us, at one time or another, picked up the 11 by 17 inch piece of paper and studied the collection of circles and squares that would be lush vegetation and an ultimate oasis in the sunny, hot Colorado summers. We seemed to know all the work that would be involved to turn the current "blank slate" into the plan on the paper.

"Wouldn't it be nice," I said at the time, "if we all had this kind of design for our lives." People responded enthusiastically; "Sign me up!" a few burst out.

What if life could be designed and drawn out for us? Not only the places where we would find shade and comfort, but also the places that would be hard and require a lot of weeding and persistence.

How much easier these places would be if we knew it was all just part of the "design" of our lives and that even the labor-intensive things would eventually lead to something beautiful.

When I started writing over ten years ago I would have never put in my design that I would self-publish a book. To me, it meant that I had somehow failed. My quest has been for all these years to not only learn to write and write beautifully, but to publish the books I write with a traditional publisher, the bigger the better, to fulfill my desire to be a "legitimate" writer. I'd be a writer who the Empire approved of, and paid handsomely. That may still happen. In fact I have a literary agent who is certain of it. But it hasn't happened as of this writing in 2008.

Seeking Sara Summers is a story that I worked on for 8 years. It came close to being bought several times by different publishers, big and small. And all along I revised and rewrote (the constant "weeding" of the writing world), honing in on the best story I could possibly write.

It is my red-headed stepchild, if I look at it in a traditional sense. But it is still a child that I love dearly and one that I have devoted many, many hours of my life to. The time came for me to time to put this creation out into the world and let it go and reach whoever it was meant to reach. Based on feedback from readers, the novel has entertained and helped those who have been searching for a more authentic life, like the main character is, and the book has encouraged them to go for it. That's just what I hoped. To write something that both inspires and encourages.

I am convinced that Life has a much bigger imagination than we do. It is designed in a way that we can't begin to comprehend and isn't that impressed with empires. Our jobs, it seems, is to simply trust the process.

Moments of Glad Grace

How many loved your moments of glad grace...

– William Butler Yeats

My mother-in-law loves this line from Yeats, and I've been having such moments of glad grace lately. I don't think I'm anything special to have them. I think we all have moments of grace. By the way, I don't think "grace" is purely a religious term. My definition would be similar to synchronicity. When something unexpected happens that makes me stop and wonder if maybe I'm not alone in this world. It's an "aha" moment. A friend stopping by with just the right words. A reader telling me what one of my books meant to him on one of those days when I'm ready to quit writing (as if I could!). A bird landing at my feet and serenading me on one of my walks. A gasp of surprise when witnessing the new life of Spring and true beauty in nature. Then realizing how fortunate I am to witness to it.

Of course, just by using the word "grace" we open ourselves up to all sorts of judgments.

Will people think we're bad, wrong, stupid or crazy? Or perhaps overly religious? Or not religious at all? Or just one of those highly imaginative artist types? The truth is that sometimes things happen that we can't explain away and that feels like a gift from some named or unnamed source. You can call that grace, good luck, good mojo, God, Goddess, whatever.

Have you had a moment of glad grace lately?

Are You Free?

"I am free, and always have been; free to accept my own reality, free to trust my perceptions, free to believe what makes me feel sane even if others call me crazy, free to disagree even if it means great loss, free to seek the way home until I find it." – Martha Beck

I like what this quote has to say. I am no stranger to great loss and you probably aren't either. I'm sure people have thought me "crazy" for seeking out what keeps me sane, for example, walks by the river in the pouring rain. But in my own way, I am in the process of finding my way home, to that deepest part of me. The part that doesn't need approval. The part that truly believes I am a good enough person/writer/friend at this moment. Yes, I believe that awareness is true freedom.

May we all be free to find our way home.

The Journey

Seth Godin's book, *The Icarus Deception: How High Will You Fly,* is all about courage, art, and why we need to fly a little closer to the sun. He writes:

Art isn't pretty.
Art isn't painting.
Art isn't something you hang on the wall.
Art might scare you.
Art might bust you.
But art is who we are and what we do and what we need.
Art isn't a result; it's a journey.
The challenge of our time is to find a journey worthy of your heart and soul.

I'm on the journey. Not only as a writer, but I am also a person who is constantly seeking the art and beauty in my life. And I think Seth is right, the journey isn't always pretty or comfortable and sometimes it's even terrifying. But as far as I'm concerned, it's the only way to go.

Have you found a journey "worthy of your heart and soul"?

Another 100 Things I'm Grateful For

It's funny how at Thanksgiving, we often focus more on the food than on what we're grateful for. I find it to be a wonderful exercise to write out 100 things I'm grateful for, whether or not it's Thanksgiving. I hope you'll try it.

Since I do this as an exercise of spontaneity, the list is not arranged in order of importance, nor is it edited.

1) my mate, my daughters, my friends
2) my 4-legged family
3) walks by the river
4) mountains
5) paths
6) movement
7) flow
8) creativity
9) bluebirds
10) blueberries
11) poetry
12) depth
13) courage
14) good stories
15) films

16) nourishing images
17) tea with a friend
18) talks about creative process
19) coffee shops
20) time to write
21) hearing from readers
22) my starred Kirkus Review
23) secrets
24) ease
25) integrity
26) metaphor
27) intuition
28) music with a muse
29) healing
30) authenticity
31) art
32) bookstores
33) honesty
34) ancestors
35) gratitude
36) connection
37) breakfast for dinner
38) organic Assam tea
39) small towns
40) community
41) trees
42) bridges

43) symbols
44) dreams
45) book sales
46) imagination
47) dancing
48) passion
49) fires in the fireplace
50) warm clothes
51) white squirrels
52) flying squirrels
53) squirrel-proof bird feeders
54) Chickadees
55) hummingbirds
56) empty nests
57) southern fiction
58) art paper
59) books
60) naps
61) working hard
62) results
63) intelligence
64) discernment
65) people that take responsibility
66) real people
67) knowledge
68) compassion
69) the color red

70) spring
71) fall
72) summer
73) winter
74) moments of certainty
75) laughter
76) ingenuity
77) a genuine smile
78) a sense of humor
79) conviction
80) hope
81) perseverance
82) rest
83) no pain
84) vision
85) hearing
86) sensation
87) words
88) images
89) tree roots above the ground
90) mountain laurel
91) river rock
92) readers
93) reviewers
94) the ability to inspire
95) real food
96) book clubs

97) word processing
98) oceans
99) curiosity
100) kindness

What Makes You Come Alive?

"Don't ask yourself what the world needs, ask yourself what makes you come alive, and then go do it. Because what the world needs is people who have come alive."
– Howard Thurman, Philosopher and Theologian

I have a challenge for you. For the next week, observe yourself to see what makes you come alive. To give you some ideas, here is my own list:

- Natural beauty—taking a walk by the mountain stream near my home

- Writing and getting into the flow of creativity where I lose track of time

- Visiting with my daughters or visiting with good friends where we talk about deep, interesting subjects

- Playing with our animal family (2 dogs, 2 cats)

- Watching a really good movie or reading a great book

- Anything that makes me laugh. I love to laugh.

What about you? What makes you come alive?

The Incredibly Messy Process of Writing a First Book

Kiran Desai is the youngest woman ever to receive the Booker Prize for her novel, *The Inheritance of Loss,* published in 2006. But she started out like everybody else with her first book called *Hullabaloo in the Guava Orchard,* not knowing exactly what she was doing and by plowing through anyway.

When asked what her writing process was like, she said:

"When I started writing it I had no idea what the story would be; I had no idea of the plot. It sort of gathered momentum and drew me along. It was an incredibly messy process and I don't know if it was the smartest way to go about it because this was my first book, so I had to teach myself how to write as I was writing it, and I don't know if I went about it the right way but I certainly had a lot of fun. It was very messy though--I had to throw out many pages--about half the book I think I ended up editing."

And:

"I think that's perhaps the hardest thing, to know when you've finished, because it seems like you can always go on polishing and polishing and working on it some more. But after a while I think I was so close to it that I couldn't even see it anymore; it didn't make sense to continue on

my own, and so I finally showed it to my agent and wanted an editor to help me take it to the next level. But, I also realized that after a point you can't go on perfecting something and polishing it and making it better, because you lose something in the process, the freshness of it, and I realized that even if it wasn't completely perfect I had to leave it; it was enough--I couldn't work on it any more. It's a balance; if you perfect one thing you lose something else, and that's the stage where I think you have to know when to stop."

So what do you think? Do you agree? Do you know when something you've written is good enough?

A Way of Life

Robert Fritz, author of *Your Life as Art*, says:

"You have good days and bad days and everything in-between. This will always be true. It is best to know this, and to know how to create on all of those days. Creating is cumulative, and is first a skill and orientation to learn, then a habit to develop, and later, a way of life and a state of being. Placing your focus on your creations rather than yourself becomes commonplace and routine, and what you think about yourself is irrelevant to anything that matters to you in your life."

As creative types, we are all on the journey of becoming a creator. Are you able to put your distractions and doubts aside in order to get the work done? Has your creativity become a "way of life and a state of being"?

What Writers and Artists Can Learn from the Rocky Mountains

As I've mentioned before, I lived in Colorado for several years and spent a lot of time in the Rocky Mountains. The snow-capped jagged peaks surrounded me like ancient grandparents who wanted to tell me their stories and pass their wisdom on to me. We have no words to describe this level of beauty. Majestic, timeless and awesome are overused. Yet every time I sat and witnessed this scene, I felt awed, refreshed and renewed.

If these mountains could talk, what would they say to artists today? (As a writer, I also consider myself an artist.) Somehow, I imagine their lessons would be about authenticity. You cannot look at these mountains and not feel their being-ness. They are solid, dependable and real.

I think writers and artists are called upon to be authentic, too. We are called upon to be observers and witnesses to our surroundings and to report back to society through our writings, paintings, sculptures, poems, and more. And I truly believe that the more real and solid we are – like the mountains surrounding us – the more effective and inspiring our work will be to others.

Perhaps these mountains would also teach us how to be unwavering in our expression of ourselves and maybe encourage us to call upon all our strength to do the work that's involved in fulfilling our purpose on this planet. Perhaps they would tell us to rest in the majestic, awesome, timelessness within, and connect to our own being-ness.

Geologists tell us that the Rockies are the second set of mountains to form in this place. The peaks of the current Rockies, soaring up to 14,000 feet and higher, were created from the remains of the ancestral Rockies from millennia before.

So, too, it seems that artists today stand on the shoulders of every artist who came before us. Not only the Michelangelos and Jane Austins, but those who did their art faithfully and honestly and were perhaps not remembered for it. Indeed, we all stand on the shoulders of giants.

Standing in the magnificent Rockies, I was reminded and re-inspired to do my work, sand grain by sand grain, to do my piece of moving humanity forward by being a writer and an artist. Please make sure you do yours, as well.

How to Stay Inspired

On Wiki-How, I came across a list of 12 things meant to help us stay inspired as writers and picked five of them as favorites. These are actually things I have done myself. See if any of these make sense for you to incorporate into your writing life.

- Create in another discipline. Artistic people have many outlets for self-expression. For example, you can balance mental projects (writing) with hands-on (crafting). It awakens different parts of the brain and forms new neural connections. Switching it up keeps the creative juices flowing.

- Always have a new project in the works. If you get discouraged with one, work on another. Experiment by changing genres, trying on different styles, writing for a different age group.

- If the muse isn't visiting, get out of the house and visit her. Make weekly art dates with yourself. Peruse book shops, galleries, concerts. Read in and out of your genre. Take a nature hike. Sketch in a coffee shop –

and eavesdrop. Inspiration is all around you. Art is ordinary life charged with meaning! Look for the beauty, the grit, the unusual, the humor, the symbolism in everyday life.

- Remember that art requires a period of gestation. Accept moments of non-productivity as the yin that goes with the yang. Something wonderful may be brewing inside. Dream. Imagine. Allow it time to take form. When you revisit your studio, you'll have a fresh infusion of energy. Always remember: the fire will return.

- Adopt a Zen-like philosophy. While you wait for agents' responses do not obsess. Focus on your art in the here and now. Artists are emotionally invested in their creations. Separate your creation from the business end. In the meantime, learn from critiques, others' wisdom, and incorporate what is useful. Keep at it, grow, improve, and... relax.

To Meander

When I lived in Colorado, heading to the Rocky Mountains was a favorite spiritual experience. A cathedral of peaks towered over us mere mortals; peaks snow-covered except for the short summer months. Moraine Park (elevation 8,000+ ft.) is the valley that runs through Rocky Mountain National Park. This valley is often full of elk herds, except for the summer when they, like people, head for higher ground and cooler temperatures.

Moraine Park also has a meander running through it. A zigzagging snake of water carrying snow-melt from the high peaks that eventually ends up in the reservoirs that feed the plains below. It is a magical place. To meander along the meander is to imitate the water leaving its impression upon the land and to imagine the force and determination the water has taken to follow its course and fulfill its purpose in the big scheme of things.

Until I lived in Colorado, I didn't realize that the word *meander* was not only a verb, but a noun. (I've led a sheltered "city" life.)

If you look up the definition of *meander* at Dictionary.com, it reads like the definition of a single individual's life journey.

1. to proceed by or take a winding or indirect course
2. to wander aimlessly; ramble
–verb (used with object)
3. *Surveying.* to define the margin of (a body of water) with a meander line.
–noun
4. Usually, **meanders.** turnings or windings; a winding path or course.
5. a circuitous movement or journey.

We don't always know where we'll end up, but we're on a journey, nonetheless. Most of us take a winding or indirect course to where we're going. Or sometimes we even wander aimlessly and ramble. But in the big scheme of things, I believe we have a purpose and any route we take works out in the end.

Writer Spends Year Walking by River

This article first appeared in the Transylvania Times on August 13, 2013.

Have you ever done something that surprised yourself, in a good way? I recently finished something that I never thought I could actually do, and I have to admit I'm kind of proud of myself. If you're in the mood for a quick story, I'd love to tell you about it.

A year ago, as I sat by a beautiful river near my home, I had what Wildflower in my latest novel would call "the secret sense," that if I didn't make some kind of grand gesture in terms of becoming more physically active (writing is very sedentary, after all), I was going to make it harder on myself down the road and perhaps even shorten my writing career. Since I have many more books I hope to write, I began to walk that same day.

The Davidson River is a picturesque river in Pisgah National Forest located in the mountains of Western North Carolina. My goal was to try to walk 365 consecutive days and experience four complete seasons of the river and surrounding forest. I made this ambitious goal about creating a relationship with this river, because I knew if I made it about losing weight or an exercise program that I would fail, as I had many times before.

Davidson River is an old friend to me. Like many people who end up settling in this area, my daughters and I used to camp by the river when they were girls and we lived in Charleston. It was where I took them for a vacation as a single mom. The campground felt safe and met our needs. That was 25 years ago.

When we moved from Charleston to Asheville in 1994, we visited even more often, walking the same trail. As the years passed, I also took anyone I cared about to Davidson River, as if introducing them to my family. It felt more like "home" to me than any place I'd ever been. (I grew up on the other side of the Smoky Mountains in Knoxville, Tennessee.) Through the late 90s and early 2000s, my dog, Grace, and I walked along this river, sometimes with friends, sometimes alone. After she died, I released her ashes where she loved to swim.

When I started my daily walks back on August 12th, 2012, I'd had years of chronic back pain and could only hobble down the trail for about 20 minutes. I had tried everything for my aching back, except surgery, but I kept hobbling, day after day. It took months and months of walking, gradually increasing my distance, but now I am up to an hour a day and I am pain free. I never thought that was even possible.

As I write this, today is day 365. I did it! To mark the occasion, friends and family gathered for a celebratory picnic by the same river.

It hasn't been easy. The weather was a constant factor, and I thought about quitting many times. We had record-setting rains in July and one of the rainiest years, in general, in decades. Needless to say, I have been making peace with mud puddles. At the same time, I have marveled at the beauty and resilience of this lush forest and the creatures that live here.

Friends have asked me if I'll continue walking now that the year is up and I always say yes. I plan to keep going, although I will probably stay home on the really bad weather days in the year to come. And even on those rare days when I may choose to stay home, I imagine the river awaiting my return.

I've written several novels, and I have thought of more than one new story I'd like to write as a result of my time spent walking by the river. It is a very fertile place for ideas.

I have also kept a river journal, where I have documented every day with observations and my progress. I may turn that into a book someday, too. If I do, you'll be the first to know.

So what began as a hope for future fitness evolved into an accidental pilgrimage. A time that proved to be incredibly challenging, as well as rich and full of creativity. At the end of my life, I imagine I will look back on this moment not only with gratitude, but with a sense of satisfaction for the year I dedicated to walking along a river.

So while I continue to be a writer, I am not a sedentary one. A river runs through my life now. With that in mind, I encourage you to consider beginning a pilgrimage of your own, whatever that may look like.

A Good Rejection?

Writing is not for the faint of heart. Nearly every step of the way involves rejection, especially if you put your work out there and want to be read. Rejections come from agents, publishers, and sometimes even readers.

Here is an example from my files of what they call in the biz a "good" rejection. How the words 'good' and 'rejection' can be used together in one sentence is questionable. But while all rejections are hard, this one was also heartening. See if you agree with me.

Dear Susan,

Apologies for taking so long to get to [your manuscript]. I read the manuscript when you first sent it, then put it away to read again later, as I wanted to think about it before looking at it again. I read it again this weekend and although there are so many things I love about it, I've come to the difficult decision to pass on it. What I love about the book is the smart, funny voice of the narrator. It would not be overstating it to say that she is reminiscent of Harper Lee's Scout. And the two lead characters are beautifully crafted. I feel like I know them quite well.

(I'll spare you the details since it hasn't been published yet and it won't make any sense to you, but it wasn't anything big or horrible. Then she kept going. Very sweet of her, actually.)

It's because I like your writing so much that I'm trying to explain this. I hope it makes sense. I'd love to read more of your work.
Thanks for letting me take a look at this. I'm sorry that in the end it wasn't right for me. I think you're hugely talented.
…..Executive Editor, [Random House imprint]

I have to admit I like the part about being "hugely talented," and any time you get compared to Harper Lee it's time to throw a party! So that's the heartening part. Still, writing takes courage and perseverance, as well as a belief in yourself and your work. Rejections are hard, no matter how *good* those rejection letters are.

What Kind of Fiction Is It?

In your work, do you fit into just one genre? Do you do just one kind of thing? Or perhaps you have diverse interests and talents?

They say it's better to specialize, have a niche, and stick to one thing. But as a writer, I am not very consistent. My first novel was contemporary fiction. My second was historical fiction and southern. Some might even call it southern gothic literature. Others might insist it is literary fiction.

I write for children *and* adults. Some of my stories are humorous and more commercial. Some have a mystery at the core. Some have a romance. A lot of them have secrets.

Most are stories about characters who come-of-age in one way or another, even if they are in their forties. Most of my characters also have courage and the ability to transcend or transform their situation. Perhaps it comes from being a psychotherapist for so many years and wishing that for my clients. As far as I know, there isn't even a name for that kind of fiction, but I like to think of it as Transformation Lit.

Unfortunately, or fortunately, I can't be pinned down and labeled easily. Can you relate?

I've written novels, short stories, flash fiction, poetry and even a play. This is how my creative process plays out. It's a wild and wonderful ride and I wouldn't change a thing. If you enjoy writing in one genre, that's great. But if you're like me and write different kinds of stories, don't worry. You are just as successful at being true to yourself and your creative process.

How Creativity Works

Jonah Lehrer, author of *Imagine: How Creativity Works* says:

"Because creativity has long been associated with the muses, we've assumed that creativity should feel easy and effortless, that if we're truly inventive then the gods will take care of us. But nothing could be further from the truth. Instead, creativity is like any other human talent – it takes an enormous amount of effort to develop. And then, even after we've learned to effectively wield the imagination, we still have to invest the time and energy needed to fine-tune our creations. If it feels easy, then you're doing it wrong."

Just like it would be impossible to take up the cello and within a few months or a year play like Yo Yo Ma, our skills at writing, singing, dancing, composing, painting, sculpting, etc., can take years to develop.

Keep in mind, this reality might be hard to wrap our minds around as members of a culture where we have been trained to expect things instantly, from messages to macaroni and cheese. Yet I haven't had anything else in my life that has proven more gratifying, more soul nourishing, than the process of developing my creative life.

What about you? Are you willing to "put in the time and energy needed to fine-tune" your creations? I hope so, because the world needs you.

The Alchemy of Revision

I am currently in the middle of the revision process for my seventh novel. I like to think of this part of the process as an alchemical process. One of the definitions of alchemy is:

"any magical power or process of transmuting a common substance, usually of little value, into a substance of great value."

The concept of alchemy is usually associated with Carl Jung who used it to describe how we develop the potential in our personalities.

Not that I think there is anything "magical" in doing three to six months of revisions. It's hard work. The first drafts of manuscripts, like the personalities of the chronically unaware, are raw, unrefined messes. To put first drafts out into the world is not only naïve but careless. They are almost always ineffective and even embarrassing when read a few years down the road. (You can also over-revise, but that's another post.) It is only in the subsequent drafts, where the true gold of a piece can be found.

In writing, excess words must be cut in order to get to the ultimate clarity of a sentence and an idea. Characters must be developed and given interesting, vital lives. Plot must be unearthed and honed into a rhythm that can sustain and carry a reader along for two to three hundred pages.

I have been writing for seventeen years. At this point I have a solid level of craft behind my revisions, as well as clear knowledge of my strengths and weaknesses. I've been to countless workshops on writing and taken creative writing classes at the university level, in addition to putting hundreds of hours into the actual process of writing. I also get the feedback of my first readers (those three or four trusted writer/friends who I let read early drafts in order to get feedback), as well as feedback from my literary agent.

The revision process is one area of my life where I am fearless. And if you are really serious about being a good writer, maybe even a great one, I think you have to be fearless, too. I have been known to throw out entire chapters if they aren't moving the plot forward. I get rid of characters without a whiff of sentimentality if they aren't compelling and holding up their end of the bargain. I change tenses if more immediacy is needed. I add new characters if they offer something unique. I add a surprise or two, perhaps a twist of fate. I do this because I am always striving for excellence when I write a story, as I am always striving for excellence in my life. I want a story to grab my readers, inspire them, and entertain them from the first to the very last page.

When I first started writing I complained a lot about the revision process. It is like putting your work onto the analyst's couch, baring its soul to find out what is genuine and what is fake. But now—and I never thought I'd say this—it is one of my favorite parts. It requires a skill set that is developed by practice, by actually writing day after day, year after year. It requires reading books on craft and going to writer's conferences with the intention of learning how to write (instead of only choosing the workshops on how to find a good literary agent). Sometimes this skill set can be developed by taking classes on writing and perhaps even belonging to a really good writers group. (The really good ones are hard to find, by the way, and may require some searching out.)

The revision process is where the most potential lives for the writer and artist. Just as increasing self-awareness is where the most potential is found in our personalities.

Revising is about becoming a master at your craft and learning how to tell a really good story or writing a really good poem or creating an awesome concerto. If you are a writer and you hate revising, then at the very least you must find yourself a freelance editor who is a good fit for you. If you are a person whose life could use some "major editing," you may want to invest in a good therapist.

The revision process is where something ordinary and mundane is transformed through the writer's own skillful efforts into something extraordinary and lasting. Whether you're revising a piece of writing or music or some non-artistic yet still creative project – or your own life – keep the faith and don't give up. Remember, you are the alchemist of your creation.

The Tenacity of Wildflowers and Writers

Sometimes as writers we can feel like we are just surviving, not thriving. Sometimes the culture we live in can be an inhospitable environment that almost seems to delight in thwarting our efforts to thrive. Let me share a quick story about the tenacity of wildflowers and what we can learn from them.

The Rocky Mountains are called the backbone of the country. They arch their peaks over 14,000 feet into the air. Trail Ridge Road traverses this exquisite landscape. It is the highest paved road in the United States, with more than eight miles lying above 11,000' and a maximum elevation of 12,183'. At its highest, the air is thin and fresh and the scenery is literally jaw-dropping. This magical place defies superlatives.

Trail Ridge Road is open from June to September. In winter, this area receives over 20 feet of snow, with drifts up to 30 feet. It takes 6 weeks of plowing the snow before the road can open. But even in summer this road can be an adventure. I have driven it in mid-June and in the span of five minutes the weather changed from intense thunder and lightning, to hail, and then snow! The alpine tundra, above tree line, and where this road takes you, is a wild and wonderful place.

In the midst of this wildness are wildflowers. Startling and breathtaking in their ability to survive in such harsh conditions, they are a perfect example of tenacity. Buried under snow for most of the year, they rush toward life in the 4-6 weeks they have every summer to fulfill their purpose. Every single bloom is a miracle.

Perhaps we writers can learn something from the tenacity of these alpine wildflowers. A lot of us go through life simply trying to survive. Many of us are buried under with work and perhaps the heavy responsibility of supporting ourselves and others, or trying to make a difference in a world that can be indifferent. Yet, like the wildflowers, we must claim the tenacity that we each possess.

We must rush toward life, and move beyond surviving to thriving.

But how do you do this? Let's take a hint from the alpine wildflowers and know that ever little bit of time we can squeeze out for our creative life is valuable. Perhaps set aside even 30 minutes twice a week to write or do your art, whatever that is. Put it in your calendar. Tell the other people in your life that this time is sacred: do not disturb.

The wildflowers make the most of an incredibly short growing season, and they return year after year to grace us with their aliveness and beauty. You can do the same.

77 Things to Do When Stressed or Uninspired

As a former psychotherapist and a current professional writer, I am well aware of how stressed, burnt out, restless, bored and uninspired this world can make us, especially if we are sensitive or creative types. Things get to us. Not because we're bad, wrong, stupid or crazy, but because we're human. As a result, we can get easily distracted from the things that really matter and—without needed rejuvenation—life loses some of its meaning and sacredness.

With that in mind, I decided to brainstorm a list of things to do when life gets hard. Sometimes small suggestions can offer big results. I invite you to come up with your own ideas, too. Here goes:

77 THINGS TO DO WHEN YOU ARE STRESSED OUT OR UNINSPIRED

1. take a walk by a body of water: river, lake, sea, stream
2. plant a small tree
3. unplug from all electronics for 24 hours
4. sit in a quiet room and close your eyes
5. make a salad of fresh fruit and eat it slowly

6. read a good book
7. write a really bad poem
8. walk barefooted in grass
9. practice laughing
10. sit on the floor cross-legged and hum
11. sit in the sun for 15 minutes
12. have a deep, meaningful conversation with a friend
13. massage your hands and feet, or have someone do it for you
14. drink a tall glass of water and think about what a gift it is to be able to swallow
15. find a swing and swing in it
16. listen to live music
17. take a novelist to lunch (I'm available on weekends :-)
18. go outside and listen to birdsong
19. plant flowers and encourage them to grow
20. yodel badly
21. hug a tree
22. let yourself cry
23. write down every cuss word you know using colored pencils
24. smile for 5 minutes without stopping (set a timer)
25. do not shop or buy anything for 24 hours
26. go to an art gallery
27. pull a random book from the fiction section of the library and read the first chapter
28. perform an anonymous and random act of kindness

29. take a mental health day at work and begin your hero's/heroine's journey
30. sing an Elvis song in the shower
31. write a letter to someone by hand and snail mail it
32. give someone flowers
33. breathe deeply 4 times: slow inhale, slow exhale
34. tell a friend 3 things you appreciate about them
35. write all your resentments on a sheet of paper and then burn them
36. go to your favorite coffee shop and speak to at least 2 people other than the barista
37. take a slow drive on a country road you've never been on before
38. make yourself your favorite meal
39. look yourself in the mirror and tell yourself: *you are good enough*
40. volunteer one afternoon in a soup kitchen
41. contact an artist (writer, poet, short story writer, novelist, painter, etc.) and tell them something you love about their work
42. count how many times you say "thank you" in one day and then double it
43. find a porch to sit on
44. donate money to an environmental or wildlife protection agency
45. play with a small child (no television allowed)
46. sit under a tree and read for 30 minutes

47. go to a farmers market and buy homegrown, fresh vegetables
48. keep a gratitude journal
49. sing a song that you used to sing as a child
50. feel blue, touch green
51. watch clouds for 30 minutes and name their shapes
52. read a fairy tale
53. listen to an audio book (after doing number 3 above)
54. make a phone call to an elderly person and tell them how much you appreciate them
55. write down your dreams
56. dance naked (your should probably do this one at home)
57. walk in the rain
58. be vulnerable with someone you can trust
59. make your own list of things to do when you feel uninspired
60. pray/meditate or walk your meditation
61. feed the birds
62. read a story to someone small or someone convalescing
63. take 4 more deep breaths and thank your body for keeping you alive
64. let your imagination run wild
65. take your intuition out for a spin
66. draw something very badly and without judgment

67. put together a box of things to give to Goodwill or another agency
68. take a nap
69. go on a news fast (no bad news) for 24 hours
70. search out stories and people that inspire you
71. play a musical instrument
72. write a song about yourself
73. go on a pilgrimage
74. attend a play
75. have a delicious dessert for dinner one night
76. while sitting quietly, ask your soul what it needs and then do it
77. read this list as often as you can

It's incredibly easy to get stressed these days and it's important to take action as soon as we realize we are anxious, bored, discouraged or distracted or our writing life may suffer.

I hope my list gave you some ideas...now make your own list of 77 things. Then pick one and do it.

Nobody will do these things for us. We have to do them for ourselves.

Never. Give. Up.

In an essay from 2011, Kathryn Stockett, author of the bestselling novel, *The Help*, said:

"If you ask my husband my best trait, he'll smile and say, "She never gives up." But if you ask him my worst trait, he'll get a funny tic in his cheek, narrow his eyes and hiss, "She. Never. Gives. Up."

She is very candid about the challenges of being a writer. She said:

"It took me a year and a half to write my earliest version of The Help. *I'd told most of my friends and family what I was working on. Why not? We are compelled to talk about our passions. When I'd polished my story, I announced it was done and mailed it to a literary agent."*

Forty rejections and a year and a half later, she got a note from an agent which read: *"There is no market for this kind of tiring writing."*

That one, she said, finally made her cry. She spent the following weekend in her pajamas wondering whether she should give up.

"But I couldn't let go of The Help," she said. *"Call it tenacity, call it resolve or call it what my husband calls it: stubbornness."*

Kathryn Stockett absolutely refused to give up.

"By rejection number 45, I was truly neurotic. It was all I could think about—revising the book, making it better, getting an agent, getting it published. I insisted on rewriting the last chapter an hour before I was due at the hospital to give birth to my daughter. I would not go to the hospital until I'd typed The End. I was still poring over my research in my hospital room when the nurse looked at me like I wasn't human and said in a New Jersey accent, "Put the book down, you nut job—you're crowning."

Then it got worse. Kathryn would sneak around to write. She confessed: *"It was as if I were having an affair—with 10 black maids and a skinny white girl."*

After her daughter was born she said she hid out in hotels on weekends to write. She could not make herself give up. By the end, she had received 60 rejections from literary agents for *The Help*. But number 61 was the one acceptance. After five years of writing and three and a half years of rejection, it only took her agent three weeks to sell the book.

"The point is," she said. *"I can't tell you how to succeed. But I can tell you how not to: Give in to the shame of being rejected and put your manuscript—or painting, song, voice, dance moves, [insert passion here]—in the coffin that is your bedside drawer and close it for good. I*

guarantee you that it won't take you anywhere. Or you could do what this writer did: Give in to your obsession instead."

Then she added:

"And if your friends make fun of you for chasing your dream, remember—just lie."

How far are you willing to go to chase your dream?

Note: The entire essay appears in the anthology *The Best Advice I Ever Got: Lessons from Extraordinary Lives*, edited by Katie Couric and published by Random House in April, 2011. Kathryn Stockett's novel, *The Help*, went on to be a bestseller and the movie premiered on August 10, 2011.

A Blessing for Writers

- May the time you find to develop your talents be sacred and abundant

- May you be surrounded by people who encourage you in small and large ways

- May you develop a tough skin and a supple heart

- May you trust your creative process and express yourself with a true and unwavering voice

- May you be rewarded financially for your efforts

- May any struggle you face make you stronger, so that you persevere and continue on the path

- May you grow in confidence, clearly seeing your value and worth

- May you be appreciated, in your lifetime, for the gift of healing you offer the world

Parting Words

Living a writing life is not easy. Because we live such busy lives and often write in stolen moments, we writers need all the encouragement and inspiration we can get. My hope is that this collection of selected writings and quotes has helped you become a more *fearless* writer. A writer who is able to take action and continue on despite the obstacles in your life. Fearlessness has its own rewards and despite the challenges of living a creative life, I highly recommend it. Truly, it can be one of the most rewarding things we ever do.

You are invited to share with me your favorite quotes and stories about creativity and the writing life. I also have a blog on my website where I post about creativity and writing.

Feel free to email me at susan@susangabriel.com. Or contact me through my author website at SusanGabriel.com and let me know your thoughts.

Lastly, I like to ask a favor. If you enjoyed this book, please consider leaving a review on Amazon or elsewhere. It really helps gets the word out to readers who are not familiar with a particular author.

Thank you for reading, and keep writing!

With every good wish,
Susan Gabriel

P.S. Do you want to get notified when I publish new books? I would be happy to email you as soon as new books are available (two to three times a year at most). Please sign up here today: https://www.susangabriel.com/new-books/

About the Author

Susan Gabriel is an acclaimed writer who lives in the mountains of North Carolina. Her novel, *The Secret Sense of Wildflower*, earned a starred review ("for books of remarkable merit") from Kirkus Reviews and was also named to their list of Best Books of 2012.

She is also the author of *Temple Secrets, Lily's Song* and other novels. Discover more about Susan at susangabriel.com

The Secret Sense of Wildflower
A novel

"A quietly powerful story, at times harrowing but ultimately a joy to read." - Kirkus Reviews

Named to Kirkus Reviews' Best of 2012

Set in 1940s Appalachia, *The Secret Sense of Wildflower* tells the story of Louisa May "Wildflower" McAllister whose life has been shaped around the recent death of her beloved father in a sawmill accident. While her mother hardens in her grief, Wildflower and her three sisters must cope with their loss themselves, as well as with the demands of daily survival. Despite these hardships, Wildflower has a resilience that is forged with humor, a love of the land, and an endless supply of questions to God. When Johnny Monroe, the town's teenage ne'er-do-well, sets his sights on Wildflower, she must draw on the strength of her relations, both living and dead, to deal with his threat.

With prose as lush and colorful as the American South, *The Secret Sense of Wildflower* is a powerful and poignant southern novel, brimming with energy and angst, humor and hope.

Available in print, ebook and audiobook editions.

Praise for The Secret Sense of Wildflower

"Louisa May immerses us in her world with astute observations and wonderfully turned phrases, with nary a cliché to be found. She could be an adolescent Scout Finch, had Scout's father died unexpectedly and her life taken a bad turn...By necessity, Louisa May grows up quickly, but by her secret sense, she also understands forgiveness. A quietly powerful story, at times harrowing but ultimately a joy to read."

– Kirkus Reviews

"A soulful narrative to keep the reader emotionally charged and invested. *The Secret Sense of Wildflower* is eloquent and moving tale chock-filled with themes of inner strength, family and love." – Maya Fleischmann, indiereader.com

"I've never read a story as dramatically understated that sings so powerfully and honestly about the sense of life that stands in tribute to bravery as Susan Gabriel's *The Secret Sense of Wildflower*…When fiction sings, we must applaud."

– T. T. Thomas, author of A Delicate Refusal

"The story is powerful, very powerful. Excellent visuals, good drama. I raced to get to the conclusion…but didn't really want to read the last few pages because then it would be over! I look forward to Gabriel's next offering."

– Nancy Purcell, Author

"Just finished this with tears streaming down my face. Beautifully written with memorable characters who show resilience in the face of tragedy. I couldn't put this down and will seek Susan Gabriel's other works. This is truly one of the best books I've read in a very long time." – A.C.

"An interesting story enhanced by great writing, this book was a page turner. It captures life in the Tennessee mountains truthfully but not harshly. I would recommend this book to anyone who enjoys historical fiction." – E. Jones

"I don't even know how to tell you what I love about this book --- the incredible narrator? The heartbreaking and inspiring storyline? The messages about hope, wisdom, family and strength? All of those!! Everything about it!" – K. Peck

"Lovely, soul stirring novel. I absolutely could not put it down! Beautifully descriptive, evocative story told in the voice of Wildflower, a young girl of the mountains, set in a wild yet beautiful 1940's mountain town, holds you captive from the start. I had to wait to write my review, as I was crying too hard to see!" – V.C.

"I write novels, too, but this writer is fantastic. The story is authentic and gripping. Her voice through the child, Wildflower, is captivating. This story would make a great movie. I love stories that portray life changing tragedy and pain coupled with power of the human spirit to survive and continue to love and forgive. Bravo! Susan. Please write more and more." – Judi D.

"This is a wonderful story that will make you laugh, cry, and cheer." –T.B. Markinson

"I was pretty blown away by how good this book is. I didn't read it with any expectations, hadn't heard anything about it really, so when I read it, I realized from page one that it is a well written, powerful book." – Quixotic Magpie

"If you liked Little Women or if you love historical fiction and coming-of-age novels, this is the book for you. Definitely add The Secret Sense of Wildflower to your TBR pile; you won't regret it." – PandaReads

"Bottom line: A great story about a strong character!" – Meg, A Bookish Affair

Temple Secrets
A novel

Fans of *The Help* and *Midnight in the Garden of Good and Evil* will delight in this comic novel of family secrets by acclaimed writer, Susan Gabriel.

Every family has secrets, but the elite Temple family of Savannah has more than most. To maintain their influence, they've also been documenting the indiscretions of other prestigious southern families, dating as far back as the Civil War. When someone begins leaking these tantalizing tidbits to the newspaper, the entire city of Savannah, Georgia is rocking with secrets.

The current keeper of the secrets and matriarch of the Temple clan is Iris, a woman of unpredictable gastrointestinal illnesses and an extra streak of meanness that even the ghosts in the Temple mansion avoid. When Iris unexpectedly dies, the consequences are far flung and significant, not only to her family—who get in line to inherit the historic family mansion—but to Savannah itself.

At the heart of the story is Old Sally, an expert in Gullah folk magic, who some suspect cast a voodoo curse on Iris. At 100 years of age, Old Sally keeps a wise eye over the whole boisterous business of secrets and the settling of Iris's estate.

In the Temple family, nothing is as it seems, and everyone has a secret.

Available in paperback, ebook and audiobook.

Praise for *Temple Secrets*

"*Temple Secrets* is a page-turner of a story that goes deeper than most on the subjects of equality, courage and dignity. There were five or six characters to love and a few to loathe. Gabriel draws Queenie, Violet, Spud and Rose precisely, with a narrative dexterity that is amazingly and perfectly sparse while achieving an impact of fullness and depth. Their interactions with the outside world and one another are priceless moments of hilarious asides, well-aimed snipes and a plethora of sarcasms. What happens when the inevitable inequities come about amongst the Haves, the Have Nots and the Damn-Right-I-Will-Have? When some people have far too much time, wealth and power and not enough humanness and courage? Oh, the answers Gabriel provides are as delicious as Violet's peach turnovers, and twice as addicting! I highly recommend this novel." – T.T. Thomas

"Susan Gabriel shines once again in this fascinating tale of a family's struggle to break free from their past. Filled with secrets, betrayals, and tragedy, the author weaves an intricate storyline that will keep you hooked." - R. Krug

"I loved this book! I literally couldn't put it down. The characters are fabulous and the story line has plenty of twists and turns making it a great read. I was born and raised in the south so I have an affinity for stories that are steeped in the southern culture. *Temple Secrets* nails it. All I needed was a glass of sweet tea to go with it." – Carol Clay

"The setting is rich and sensuous, and the secrets kept me reading with avid interest until most of them were revealed. I read the book in just a few days because I really didn't want to put it down. It is filled with characters who are funny, tragic, unpredictable and nuanced, and I must admit that I really came to know and love some of them by the end of the story."
– Nancy Richards

"I was glued from the first moment that I began reading. The book accurately portrays many of the attitudes of the Old South including the intricate secrets and "skeletons in the closet" that people often wish to deny. Each character is fascinating and I loved watching each one evolve as the story unfolded. This was one of those books that I did not want to finish as it was so much fun to be involved in the action."
– Lisa Patty

"I just finished reading *Temple Secrets* today and I truly hated for it to end! Susan Gabriel writes with such warmth and humor, and this book is certainly no exception. I loved getting to know the characters and the story was full of humor and suspense." – Carolyn Tenn

Available in print, ebook and audiobook editions.

www.ingramcontent.com/pod-product-compliance
Lightning Source LLC
LaVergne TN
LVHW041250080426
835510LV00009B/665